Forgetting
JL Brooks

FORGETTING
Copyright © 2014 by JL Brooks

Dedication

I wrote this book for numerous reasons...

For those who have suffered with mental illness

For those who have battled with cancer

For those who give their lives to take care of the fighters

For those who fight for our freedom

For those who have ever lost someone they loved

For those who feel as though they have never been loved

This is for you

YOU ARE LOVED!!!

&

For Shana Shaffer-Ficks, the most incredible fighter I have ever met.

For Mylee Cardenas.

And for Dr. Vincent Tuohy at the Cleveland Clinic, the creator of the Breast and Ovarian Cancer Vaccine. Yes it exists. Yes it works. So why haven't we heard more about it? Because there is no money in a cure. It is sad but true. But we can make a difference. Where others have said no, we can say yes. A portion of the proceeds of this book is going directly to his research, and I will use my voice in any way possible to let others know that there is hope. You can donate directly to his work and know that every dollar will be used to bring it forth at a more rapid pace.

"We believe that this vaccine will someday be used to prevent breast cancer in adult women in the same way that vaccines prevent polio and measles in children," says Dr. Tuohy.

To learn more and to make a donation, please visit:

http://giving.ccf.org/site/PageServer?pagename=vaccine

"You are the light of the world. A town built on a hill cannot be hidden. Neither do people light a lamp and put it under a bowl. Instead they put it on a stand, and it gives light to everyone in the house. In the same way, let your light shine before others, so they may see your good deeds, and glorify your father in heaven."

~Matthew 5:14-16

Dear Reader

Before you begin, I want to share something with you. From the beginning of time, people have used stories as a way of teaching others important life lessons in a way that can easily be remembered and passed along to others. This method of preserving information is hard wired into our very being for a reason, to prevent forgetting. The only way it can be lost, is to stop telling the story. Books can be destroyed, photos can vanish, and your digital memories are only able to be retrieved with the proper equipment and electricity. What remains eternal is your story. And not even death has the power to affect that truth.

If you are to remember one single thing from our time together, is that we are all connected, linked forever into what is known as history. Life is a blank page of opportunity, and within all of us is the ability to write our futures. From this perspective, I ask you to stop and reflect for a moment on what story you want to tell. It is never too late to change how it ends. It all comes down to choice.

On October 7th, 2014, I made the decision to do a radio

show about breast cancer where I was paired with the brilliant Mylee YC. I knew nothing about her before that night, and afterwards, I understood even more in how the universe conspires on your behalf to tell an amazing story. And you dear reader, can help us write it.

I am going to let Mylee tell you who she is. But first, I will tell you a little about who I really am. By day I am a women's health educator and advocate. My best friend is a cancer survivor who was diagnosed with Stage 2 breast cancer while she was 6 months pregnant. It is she who I traveled the dark road with, and witnessed first-hand how hopeless it can feel. In turn, it also let me see what so many others are up against. The only weapon I possess in this fight is my ability to share stories. Yet I understand the true meaning of the quote, "the pen is mightier than the sword". It was my writing that has lead me to this moment, to Mylee, and to countless others in this fight.

Our intention, is together, use this story as one vehicle to reach others who feel that there is no one fighting on their behalf. To "rally the troops" and help us spread the word that there is hope. Alone we are but one flame, together we can light up the world. We invite you to not just read a story, but join us in writing history. By simply purchasing this book, part of your money has gone to support Dr. Vincent Tuohy's ground breaking research, which you read about and can learn more from the dedication page. You are also helping to support grassroots efforts to support men and women emotionally, spiritually, mentally and physically. By giving our voices power, it ripples out to others who are in the trenches fighting for those we love, and to those that need our help. Thank you is not enough.

Now I would like for you to meet Mylee YC...

Hello Everyone,

My name is Mylee Cardenas and I am so honored to be writing this letter. I met J.L when we did a radio show about breast cancer together. Right away I could tell that we both shared a passion for sharing information and experience to help others. J.L. reached out to me after the show to continue our dialog. She has a heart of gold and a desire to make a difference in this world. During the show J.L. mentioned the work she was doing with Dr. Vincent Tuohy, I was intrigued given the fact that he has created a vaccine that could prevent so many other women from future diagnosis of breast or ovarian cancer. Needless to say J.L. and I bonded quickly and found that we both wanted to do something about this.

Before I jump onto my soapbox let me tell you a little about myself. I am a single mom of an amazing little girl who is my world and my best friend. For 12 years I served in the US Army as direct support to Special Operations Teams. After joining at 17 the Military quickly became my passion as well as our family. I loved almost everything about it and I felt as though I was very good at my job. In 2011 I was part of an amazing group of women selected to do a new job working and living with spec ops teams at the village level in Afghanistan. This was the height of my career for me and I felt like I was finally where

I needed to be. I was constantly being challenged and learning new things, which was exciting to me. We deployed in August and after my first mission I knew that I had found my path.

In November 2011 after returning from a mission I discovered a mass that was about the size of a golf ball. I didn't think much of it because of where were located. I thought maybe it was a boil or worst case a fluid filled cyst from all the vaccines and medications they had us on. I decided to watch it and continue the mission. By January it had grown into the size of a ping-pong ball and was quite hard, I began to get a bit concerned but still did not want to make a big deal about it. I had worked so hard to earn the respect of the people I worked with and I didn't want it to look like I was looking for a way out. Beside what if I was medically evacuated to Germany and it turned out to be nothing? I would never live it down, so I waited and finished my tour.

Upon returning home I went off post and paid for an ultrasound this led to my diagnosis of Stage 3c Invasive Ductal Carcinoma. The military moved my daughter and I to a new base where I really only knew a couple people and I started treatment. It was not an easy road I had an aggressive treatment plan; Chemotherapy, Bilateral Mastectomy, dissection of my axilla (with removal of 22 lymph nodes), partial hysterectomy, expansion, reduction, max dose of Radiation, and expansion again. Through all of this I was alone with my daughter, my unit had decided that I was a "problem child" and they became "impatient with my illness". Over the past 12 years I had developed my own way of coping with trauma and stress. No matter what I would analyze it deal and just push though.

After the organization (military) I loved the most turned on me I was forced into facing what I viewed as "weaknesses" So in the mist of fighting my Cancer I was diagnosed with severe PTSD related to the Cancer, Combat, and a brutal physical and sexual assault from 2009 that I never dealt with. Life was a mess but I did my best to keep it together because anything less would have felt like failure.

I am so new to this world of speaking out and having a voice so I still struggle with what to say and I wonder if I am saying the right things. I realized over the past few years that all I can do is share my experience because I really could have used that while going through everything. When you are going through a traumatic situation everything is a challenge and you can either step up and fight back or just go along for the ride. I am so not that person I fought back by educating myself and no matter how terrible things seemed I would find one positive thing to hold on to everyday. I still struggle with my PTSD and

I am still dealing with this Cancer thing but I refuse to let this beat me. I will win through educating myself, staying healthy, focusing on the positives and finding ways to keep living to the fullest. My goal is to not let my experiences just be my experiences. I want to share them in hopes that they will help someone know that they can overcome whatever it is they are facing and that they are not alone.

Which brings me here. When J.L. sent me her book to read I was not only honored but I was excited to see the type of writer she was. You can tell a lot about a person through their writing. The story was amazing and very relatable. You have this story about this tough woman that does not let anyone see any weakness. And then she is stripped down to the most vulnerable she has ever been. As I read it I thought "yup been there". There were so many highs and lows throughout that I went back and re-read it to make sure I didn't miss anything. As you are reading this story you will think about the struggle, about love and about the true nature of the human spirit. All of the things that make us human are what make us strong and able to bounce back from a dark place and find ourselves.

Life is so full of the uncontrollable factors and sometimes no matter how hard it may be we have to let go of the past and just exist in the present. We have to try to understand how strong we really are and to give ourselves the permission to move forward and keep fighting for the life our dreams. In a perfect world we would get to choose what happens to us however, this is far from a perfect world. We have to take it all the good, the bad, the ugly and the true. I have been telling myself for the past 3 years "I may not have control over a lot but I do have control over how I think, how I feel and what I do."

Action speaks louder than words and I am proud of the work that J.L. is doing and I want to thank you all for purchasing this book. J.L. is donating a portion of the book sales to help fund Dr. Tuohy's research. I believe this vaccine should be available to the public but as J.L. says there is no money in a cure. It infuriates me to hear this but it is the truth. So I would like to challenge you all to share Dr. Tuohy's donation page, do your own fundraisers or whatever we can to help make this vaccine available to the public. Think of it this way a vaccine for the people by the people. Can you imagine a grassroots funded vaccine? Cut out the middle man, if the government or pharmaceutical companies won't give him the money then let's raise it. If this vaccine could keep my daughter from ever having to go through all this then I will be upfront leading the charge. It's all about action…..Dr. Tuohy took action in dedicating himself to creating this vaccine to prevent breast and ovarian cancer, J.L. is working to raise awareness and money to help fund this vaccine and now it is our turn.

I cannot thank J.L. enough for working as hard as she does and also for giving me the privilege to speak to all of you. Thank you for reading this and thank you for your help in this mission to support Dr. Tuohy. I cannot wait to see what we can do together for the future this vaccine.

"Yesterday I did, today I can, tomorrow I will"

~Mylee Cardenas

Thank you for taking a moment and letting us share a piece of our story, before you dive into this. A fun fact is that Forgetting was written before Mylee and I were introduced. Sometimes in our lives, something so profound happens, you cannot help but know it is bigger than you. Miracles still happen every day. I want you to take a look in the mirror and smile, because you are one of them.

With love,
J.L. Brooks

Table of Contents

Chapter 1

~ What Goes Up ~

I loved this town. Despite the hordes of celebrities crawling around Utah in the quaint but luxurious village of Park City, nestled within the Wasatch Mountains and bursting with the distinct kind of charm I savored. Perhaps it was because it reminded me so much of home. The full moon illuminated the powder-covered giants looming all around. Soft yellow lights twinkled in a haze as delicate snowflakes swirled in the howling breeze. While most of those here for the annual film festival partied far up in the extravagant log mansions owned by the uber-wealthy, I preferred the low-key rooms of the Washington School House.

It was a renovated historic building, nothing frivolous, but absolutely elegant and right in the heart of town. It was small enough that I could slip in and out unnoticed, and was my new favorite place to stay. While sitting at the window to smoke, I couldn't help but shiver a bit as the cold wind bit through the sheer T-shirt I was wearing. Shaking slightly, I took in one last drag before dropping the butt in a beer bottle and blowing the smoke out through the drapes. The crackling fire did little to warm my bones, yet I leaned in and held my hands as close to the flames as I could without singeing the skin. Watching the young man in my bed with the perfect features sleeping so peacefully, I decided to give him another moment in his dreams before I would violently crash them down.

My fingertips danced along his shoulders, drawing a sweet smile from him as he rolled over and pulled me close.

"Damn, Stella. You were incredible tonight. Why aren't you sleeping?"

I pushed my fingers a little firmer into his skin to rouse him more.

"I don't sleep. In fact, I have things I need to do soon, so I need you to get up. A driver is waiting downstairs to take you to the airport."

As he sat up slightly and rubbed his face, I could see the confusion ripple across.

"Leave? I just got here. The festival is on for a few more days. I thought we would be seeing some premiers."

I walked over to the window again and cracked it wide, then lit up another cigarette and inhaled deeply. I normally didn't smoke this much, but I hated the awkward moments when I was forced to kick someone out of my room.

"The festival is going on for a few more days, but you, my dear, are leaving. If you choose not to, you must make other arrangements for the remainder of your stay. You were here on a job, which was to be my arm candy. If your agent did not make that clear, my apologies, I suggest you get a new agent."

Joshua continued to reel from the rude awakening, looking hurt at his dismissal. I wanted to feel bad, but I was actually being nice. My kindness was feeling short lived, as occasionally these boys did not get the hint. One would think that the opportunity to bang a rock star would be enough, but sometimes they got a little too starry eyed, forcing me to live up to my nickname in certain circles. *Fly Trap*. I liked it so much I had a small tattoo of the carnivorous plant on the inside of my hipbone as a warning.

Without another word, he searched the room for his belongings and packed his suitcase. Standing quietly awaiting direction, his pitiful demeanor made me angry, not remorseful as it may someone else. I walked over to him and roughly grabbed his crotch with my left hand and his hair with my right. As I jerked both swiftly, he grunted, yet did not fight.

"If you have any hope of making it in this world, don't ever let anything grab you by the balls the way that I am right now. Remember you are a fucking man, now act like one. Get out of my fucking room, I'm done with you." I spat.

I held the door open and ushered him out, but stopped him just before he crossed the threshold. I gently grabbed hold of his chin, kissed his quivering lips, and whispered in his ear, "Goodbye, Joshua."

Sadly, he was just the beginning. Nothing about the morning was unusual. Accused of being heartless on more than one occasion, I found it much easier to treat men as if they only existed for my entertainment. Twisting my wrist, the firelight intensified the small key etched into my skin. Recalling a time long ago when I actually gave a shit, the key served as a reminder of why I never submitted to anyone, ever, especially when it came to love.

I fell once and never recovered. Each time I found myself drawing close, I took another trip to the tattoo parlor and reminded myself of why it was a tragic sentiment. The body was a temporary vessel, which I could give easily without thought. Counting down the days until I ended up in the grave, I sought to distill every moment of pleasure imaginable. If not between the sheets, there wasn't anything a bottle of tequila or a rail of cocaine couldn't achieve.

This was the cycle I lived repeatedly. If I had the privilege of being anonymous it wouldn't be such a hassle, but one careless image of me in a compromising position could damage my reputation in a way I couldn't afford. My reputation preceded me, and I did a damn good job of making sure there was never proof. The agents knew I chewed these boys up and spit them out, yet eagerly accommodated every request. Vida, my manager-slash-partner in crime, earned every penny making sure it all looked flawless, even when I wasn't sure what day it was. She was the savviest bitch I knew, and I trusted her with my life. Before sliding my keycard into her door, I pressed my ear against it to make sure she wasn't mid-coitus— though I have purposely walked in on her a few times to scare the men she'd seduced for the night.

Hearing nothing, I gently pried the door open and saw her hand waving at me as she lay sandwiched between two well-muscled bodies.

"You are such a whore, I love it." I laughed quietly.

I slid myself up behind one of the men, who I knew would be absolutely delectable. Vida didn't slum. We had different taste, but I would often see them doing the walk of shame . . . or should I say pride. From what I've seen and heard, Vida was a fuck you never forgot or denied.

I tried my hardest not to laugh as I skimmed my hand across his naked chest and down to his groin, freezing when it reached his erection. Knowing where it had been, I wiped my hand on his thigh, causing him to roll over. Surprised when he opened his eyes to someone other than Vida, he jolted for a second, then smiled broadly when he realized who I was. Fuck, he was gorgeous. If he hadn't just nailed my friend, I would be half tempted to snag him for myself. Messy blond hair tousled perfectly against bronzed skin that peeked through the colorful palate inked across his chest and limbs, and a beautiful smile of blinding white teeth. He looked familiar, but I couldn't place him.

As if reading my thoughts, Vida spoke up, saying, "He's Kai, the drummer for Mistaken Identity."

I raised my eyebrows and pursed my lips. That's where I knew him from. My band Protest had done a show with them a few months back and I had a fling with the lead singer, Levi. I was curious as to who was on the other side, and a small part of me was really hoping it wasn't him. I couldn't imagine guys in the same band tagging a girl together, but then again, I had been known to do some weird shit with my crew.

"Who's over there?" I pointed to the body on the other side of Vida.

Kai cringed a little and shrugged his shoulders.

With wide eyes, I mouthed, "Seriously"?

He gave a devious grin. I could have had a lot more fun with him than I did with the kid.

As he pulled me closer into his arms, I shook my head. "You should have waited; you could have had me instead." I pouted my lips and tried to act indifferent.

Not giving in, he continued to squeeze me tighter to him, making his arousal known.

"No, no, no, Don Juan. I don't do sloppy seconds."

Vida must have grown annoyed with our conversation, because she used her legs to shove Kai, kicking us both off the bed, with me landing on my back and him above me.

"Owe! What the fuck was that for?" I looked to Kai for an explanation, but Vida rolled over and looked pissy from her perch.

"He was waiting for you, hoebag. He wouldn't fuck me."

Looking up, I stared at the gorgeous man skeptically for confirmation. "Um, so why are you naked if you didn't do the nasty?"

He chuckled hard while keeping me pinned beneath him and smiled at Vida. "Because she told me that you would be getting into bed with us and I better be ready. I thought she was talking shit, but I couldn't risk the chance. Sure enough, here you are."

I smiled lazily and reached my fingers up to run through his hair. "Good boy. Get your pants on. You're coming with me."

"Yes, ma'am," he replied with pleasure.

For the next few hours, we created a song so loud and obnoxious, Kai and I were asked to leave the hotel. Vida was none too pleased, as she knew it would hit newsstands and tabloid magazines within a few hours. I was supposed to be snowboarding solo for the rest of the day, but plans changed. Kai was dying to tackle the slopes, and jumped at the chance to attempt my favorite run. Portuguese Gap was an exquisite double black diamond that never failed to get my heart pumping. With my tolerance to things that excited me growing dim, I was always looking for ways to enhance the rush, and Kai was happy to join the party. Pushing far enough away from the crowd to avoid our actions being too obvious, I pulled the small vial necklace out of my jacket and twisted off the plastic lid attached to a metal spoon. Holding my hand gently around it to prevent the powder from blowing away, I took a scoop and offered it up before taking two of my own and giving him one more.

Our teeth gritted eagerly between the cocaine and the rush of what we were about to do. Licking my finger, I coated it with a little more coke and rubbed it across his lips before kissing him deeply. "Let's do this!"

Snapping our boots to the boards, I went first and screamed loudly as I dashed down the side of the peak, sliding back and forth as the trees raced by me. I was unable to see how far behind Kai was, but I didn't care; the feeling of soaring through the air was all that mattered. My heart felt like it was about to burst from beating so hard, and my bones wanted out of my body. I almost couldn't handle the surge of adrenaline. I loved every second of it, because I felt alive.

I came to a place where I could stop and watch as Kai careened down the run with just as much enthusiasm as I'd had. His presence was completely unexpected, but thoroughly welcome. Although we had known each other for a grand total of about four hours, our lifestyles gave us a sense of kinship not found elsewhere. He did not know me, but he got me. He did not have to ask questions, because he already knew. There were no strings or awkwardness. We simply were, and it felt almost as good as the cocaine coursing through my veins.

He approached me with that same devilish grin, which he dropped quickly as he came to a stop. "Fuck, Stella. Your nose . . ."

As he reached into his pockets to look for something, I wiped my hand under my nostrils and studied the thick crimson liquid soaking the fabric. My face was so numb I had failed to feel the blood pouring down. The sound of a twig snapping stole my attention. Thinking it was a deer or animal in the woods, I glanced over and quickly realized I was wrong. "Fuck, fuck, fuck . . . three o'clock." I coiled my head toward Kai's chest and started to shake while pinching my nose.

I heard him growl loudly while rubbing my back. Reaching underneath his jacket, he ripped part of his tee-shirt off and wadded it into a rag for me to wipe my face.

"Damn it! Kai, I'm sorry, you should go. You don't need to be a part of this. I can explain it later. High altitude, nose bleeds, shit happens all the time. Really, it's cool."

I was lying through my teeth, making up a story about high altitudes when really it was from the drugs flowing through me.

"Stella, you're crazy if you think I am going to leave you like this. Let's get you down the mountain."

I looked up into his hazel eyes. His pupils were enlarged, even against the glare of the snow, and he smiled.

"Thank you."

He held my face gently and wiped a little where some blood must have smeared. I removed the cloth and looked at him with hope. "Yes? No? Am I good?"

He took the cloth and pressed it up to my nose again. "No, it's still going. Here, try this." Kai ripped a little more from his shirt into two small balls of fabric and encouraged me to shove them into my nose as temporary plugs. It wasn't exactly comfortable, but it had to do. Before going down, I sent Vida a text and told her that a paparazzi was on the hill, I had a nose bleed, and she needed to find out who it was and get it taken care of. Before she could respond, I shoved my phone in my pocket and refastened my boots.

I refused to look at the camera and moved as quickly as I could past him. Upon hearing the motor of the snowmobile start up, I shouted over to Kai and pointed. There was no one out here to protect us. This wasn't like being somewhere I could go and hide. This asshole had a fucking snowmobile, and was chasing us down like animals. *One day of peace, one day of fun. One day I want to be fucking normal again.* No sooner had the thought crossed my mind than I turned to look at Kai—but he wasn't there. I screamed his name, but heard nothing back. The world went black.

Chapter 2

~ The Great Pretender ~

"I don't know what makes these rock stars think they are so damn invincible. They have the same flesh and blood as us normal folk. One day they are trashing a penthouse at some swanky hotel, next day they are in a hospital bed getting their asses wiped by people like us." The woman's voice was harsh and full of sarcasm, though what it had to do with me I wasn't sure. At first it was muffled, but then it became a little clearer. I thought I'd heard my mom talking to someone earlier, but it wasn't me. It had been seven hours since I woke up, if that's what you call it. The only reason I knew that was the radio playing soft classical music and the announcer stating the time every few songs. I wanted to scream, but nothing would move, not even my eyelids. It wouldn't do much good, anyway. I could tell I was hooked up to a ventilator, and there was a small tube running down my nose. Every time I swallowed, the muscles in my throat constricted around it. I wanted to cough, but once again, zilch. I had so many questions. What happened? Why was I here? I knew it was some hospital, and something was wrong.

I didn't want to believe this was permanent, being able to hear everything around me but not respond. It had been less than half a day, and I already wanted to die. I couldn't cry, couldn't do anything. I started to feel the fingers that touched me as they took my pulse and changed my bedding. The sheer embarrassment of soiling myself without any control was the worst. The only thing that made it any better was going back and thinking about the last thing I could remember.

My mom and I had just been in a fight.

Yet that, too, was dismal.

She'd received this great opportunity to take over a private practice in Mooresville, North Carolina. She found a house right on Lake Norman, and apparently, several famous race car drivers lived nearby. However, it was my senior year of high school. I wanted my mom to be happy, and this is what she had been spending her whole life working toward, so I didn't have a choice. I had to go. My father was an elder at our church and found another parish to take him in, so there was nothing to stop us. We were supposed to be moving in a few weeks. Summer was just beginning, and I couldn't remember leaving yet.

My heart was breaking, thinking about all of my friends that would graduate together. Starting over somewhere new so late scared me. I would not have the teams I had played soccer and cheered with for years. No best friends. No boyfriend. I was alone.

All those things seemed so trivial at the moment, since I could not even breathe on my own. It was hard to tell if I was awake or asleep. I was praying this was a dream, but I knew it wasn't. Hearing the time again, I realized the nurses should have been on their next rounds. Just then, at 6:14, the door clicked and soft footing glided along the floor toward me. I felt a little jerking on the tube before the cool liquid poured down into my stomach. I had not felt it before now. She pressed the stethoscope onto my inner elbow and the chill caused a shiver through my bones that hurt.

Canon in D Minor came on; the song so many walk down the aisle to when they get married. I felt tears rush to the surface. Knowing that day would probably never come for me ripped at my gut. As the violins got stronger, the tears pooled and fell down the sides of my face, dripping into my ears. It was uncomfortable, yet for the first time that day, it was a sweet victory. I could actually feel something from within.

Throughout the night, I savored every nerve that began to come alive in my body. I still could not move, but I could feel. In the beginning, it came in slight twitches, and then eventually, I was able to will a more forceful jerk. At 10:13 in the morning, my eyes finally opened. The light was blinding, and I immediately shut them before slowly cracking them open again. I took my time to look around the room to assess my surroundings, and my eyes widened in horror at the ink-covered limbs covered in medical tape and heplocks.

This wasn't my body.

I didn't have tattoos.

This was some horrible nightmare, like the Twilight Zone, a really bizarre dream or hallucination. I could close my eyes for only so long once I had opened them. I didn't understand. When the nurses would come in, I pretended to sleep. I wasn't ready to find out what kind of freak existence I had become conscious in.

A sharp pain tore through my head, triggering some type of alarm. My heart rate must have elevated as a team rushed into the room.

"We have a response, she's waking up. Stella, can you hear me?" Loud snapping and shouting came from all around. My eyelids were ripped open, aiming a bright beam of light shining down in them.

"Pupils dilating. We need to calm her down. Blood pressure dropping, she's going into shock."

Shock? Why would I go into shock? Before I could think much more, a warmth crept through my veins and over my confusion. The black abyss I had grown to know so well opened up and took me under once more.

I wasn't sure how much time had passed, but when I awoke, I was no longer hooked to the ventilator. The NG tube, however, was still shoved down my nose. I willed my fingers to curl, and to my surprise, they did. I could move.

I lifted my arms and brought them closer to my face to inspect the designs etched into them. Once I got past the hysteria of my condition, I realized the tattoos were beautiful. They had to be mine, as colorful gladiolus flowers wrapped around in a bouquet of multicolored ink on one arm. Additional random depictions looked like they told a story I didn't remember. On the other arm, angels and demons wrestled amid stars and other celestial objects.

Anger at my incoherence took over and I wanted out of the bed, away from the hospital, and to find answers to why things were this way. I slowly pulled the tube out of my nose, and gagged as it slid out of my throat. Realizing I was hooked up to a monitor, I reached over to turn it off so it would not sound an alarm, but I misjudged the distance and fell onto the hard concrete floor. Surely enough, the alarms sounded. Several nurses came in and immediately moved me back into the bed. I could not pretend I wasn't awake any longer. A battery of questions came at me and once again, my head began to hurt. I could shake my head and nod, but had not tried to speak. The small bursts of motion were exhausting.

A doctor came in and quickly realized I was overwhelmed. He asked everyone to leave, then dimmed the lights and took a seat in the recliner to the left of the hospital bed. He introduced himself as Dr. Gleason, a neurologist at Park City Medical.

"I know you have a lot of questions, Stella, and we will answer them all to the best of our abilities, but you need to be patient. First, I have a few questions, is that okay?"

I nodded my head, tired, yet eager to find out what was going on.

"Okay, good. We will start out slowly," he said as he opened a small laptop and began typing. He asked all the basic questions. How old are you? Do you know what year it is? Do you know why you are here?

His face stilled for a moment as I tried to respond. I could feel my brain telling the muscles in my mouth to move, but nothing would come out. My eyebrows furrowed and my jaw began to quiver in frustration at my inability to communicate.

Dr. Gleason smiled and gently placed his hand over mine. "It's okay, Stella. You are already showing remarkable progress. Sometimes certain motor skills take a bit longer to come back. I have noticed you move your arms; do you think you could tap on a button?"

I calmed down a bit, and my eyes widened when I saw him remove the screen from his laptop. Never before had I seen a person touch a screen, much less a laptop you could take apart. I hesitated, and looked to him for confirmation that he wanted me to touch the tablet that held multiple keys and buttons in the window.

"Stella, tell me what year it is."

I reached up to tap the screen, which responded to my fingertips with a slight vibration. I jerked back after the first one, but he encouraged me to continue. Slowly, my shaking hand pressed in the current year: 1997.

I did not have to see his face to know I gave the wrong answer. He remained silent and asked if I knew where I was. Typing in Ohio was also incorrect, as he had stated earlier, and his badge confirmed, that we were in Park City. He stopped asking questions and put the screen back on the keyboard to type a few more things before setting it down.

In a practiced voice, he calmly gave me the news I was dreading, the truth. "Stella, I know this may be hard to hear, but you are not seventeen. You are thirty-three years old. The year is two thousand thirteen. You were in a snowboarding accident. You hit a tree and suffered a major blow to the head. For the past two weeks, you have been in a coma. Do you remember any of that?"

Shaking my head furiously, the screams that had been contained finally found a way out and rattled my body as they moved, evoking the growls of the monsters that lived in my skull. Now I knew this was a dream. I was not in an accident. That was impossible. The tattoos on my body were not real. The anger once again caused a headache unlike anything I had experienced before. Grabbing my head, my hands prickled against the short stubbly growth and roughness of thick skin sewn together.

A large area of my head had been shaved. I'd had surgery. This was not a dream. I could feel the sutures with my fingertips. "Make it stop," I graveled out of my throat to the calm doctor. The first words I would speak would be a prayer of mercy. Knowing the pain I was in, he kindly injected more drugs into my IV line and let me slip into that thoughtless place.

My mother was at my side as my eyes cracked open once more to the nightmare I couldn't change. Time must have passed because she was different. Her hair was highlighted, whereas I remembered she always wore it in a chocolate-brown hue. Her skin was sun kissed, as if she had been gardening all day, a little too pink on the cheeks. Although she had aged, she was still the most beautiful woman I knew. Dr. Alessandra Brady once had a prestigious spot as the director of Neonatology at Columbus Children's Hospital. Her passion for working with infants ran deep, but as she grew older, she had longed to spend more time with my father in a less hectic environment.

Right now, she was not looking at me as a patient, but it did not stop her from checking every chart and monitor in my room. She was a bit demanding on the staff as they administered my medications. She watched like a hawk, and commented on everything. After I sobbed uncontrollably at her presence, she refused to leave my side. Within five hours, she had negotiated my release and transport to North Carolina. I said very little as everything whirled around me like a tornado. Although I had awakened, I was still merely an observer to a life I did not recognize.

Expecting to drive to an airport, I was confused when the elevator ascended to the top level of the hospital and a nurse wheeled me out to the hospital's helipad. Dr. Gleason opened the door for my mother, and then helped move me into a seat. I knew that the doctor would be traveling with us until I was admitted to the hospital in Charlotte. We traveled a short distance to a small airport where a jet was waiting for us. Inside the cabin, it was luxurious beyond belief.

Even the doctor whistled while boarding and gave me a wink. "I should have been a singer, not a doctor." He said.

Giving a confused stare, my attention was drawn to another person joining us on the flight. An extremely tall man in a black wool jacket and olive green hat bent low and walked cautiously towards me before taking the adjacent seat. His bright blue eyes were even brighter against the moisture pooling in the corners, visible even behind the thick black frames of his glasses. I attributed it to the freezing chill and thought nothing more of it. He was younger than the others, but even more serious in stature. His mouth was pulled tight and he never once took his eyes off of me. I had seen him in the hospital talking to my mother and assumed he was assisting with my transport.

I broke the awkward connection and glanced around while being strapped into a plush leather seat and reclined back. My mother sat near me with Dr. Gleason, reviewing charts on computers and discussing my care, without explaining his comment or mentioning why we were on a private plane.

"We cannot determine how much damage has occurred. She has the ability to be vocal, yet she's choosing not to. It is most likely fear, as she believes it's almost twenty years ago and she's in Ohio. Something about that point in her life was a catalyst. Do you know what it could be?"

"I do," my mother whispered softly. "We moved that year. She was forced to leave her friends and the life she knew. It was really hard on her; she basically had to form a new identity. You know, we should really wait until she is asleep to discuss these things. I don't want her to be overwhelmed any more than she already is."

Dr. Gleason agreed with her, and they switched to the topics of physical therapy, cognitive testing, referrals, and the best drug treatment options. The man across from me stayed vigilant, which piqued my curiosity. However, nothing made sense, so I did the only thing I could to be okay; I closed my eyes and pretended none of this was happening.

Chapter 3

~ Mother Knows Best ~

I had finally come to terms with the fact I had been in an accident and suffered a brain injury. I retained all of my motor skills and resumed the ability to walk after several weeks of physical therapy. It may have been more difficult to accept if the damage had been worse. I could not change my situation, so I tried to make the best of it. Initially, I refused to accept the diagnosis. One day, during a fit of rage, I cut off the rest of my hair. My father kept his clippers in the bathroom closet, and I found them while learning where everything was. Because I was in a wheelchair, I was unable to see most mirrors. I tried to avoid them at all cost anyway, because I was terrified by my reflection. The bleached blond locks that still hung past my shoulders looked out of place with the massive area of hair missing from the surgery. Why they had not shaved my head entirely was a mystery.

My mother had raced in as soon as she heard the distinct buzz of the clippers, and watched the handfuls of hair that fell all around me. With tears strewn down both of our faces, she gently took the clippers out of my hand and finished what I had started. After pouring a warm bath, she helped me move into the water and sat next to me, holding my hand as more tears poured down. As if I were a child, she washed my back and feet, then behind my neck and knees. She knew I hated being so weak, as I had inherited her fierce nature.

"Stella, I know this is hard, but trust me that it will be okay. You are home now, where I can take care of you. It will not be long before you are out in the world again, where you won't need anyone, including me."

She sounded so wistful, making me question her comment. "You are my mother, I will always need you. Why would you say that?"

She stopped rubbing the soapy sponge across my back and dipped it into the water while collecting her thoughts. "You are just a strong-willed woman. I know you will thrive soon enough."

I could tell by her tone that there was something behind her hesitancy. I was in no position to prod, yet in that moment, I resolved to find out exactly what kind of person I was before all of this occurred. I gave it a few days before approaching the topic. It would turn out that I would not need to bring it up; it would surface on its own. Two days later, my mother was preparing to attend a homebirth. Being a partner in a small practice gave her control in a way a hospital never could. Despite her initial reservations, she had come to know the area's midwives and respect the decisions of the more holistic practices people preferred. Her lack of judgment made her trusted, so when she felt that more drastic measures should be taken, the townspeople were more willing to accept treatment.

I followed her into her office as she began to work on her computer and check her supplies. As she was typing away, I mindlessly pulled items out from the bag and organized them. Talking to myself, I listed them off while gently tucking each item back in. "Gloves, fetoscope, flashlight, suturing set, oxygen, ambu bag." Only after the zipper was pulled did I stop and realize what I had done.

"Why are you crying, Mom?"

My fears were put to ease as she wrapped me tightly in her arms. "You are coming back, Stella. You may not realize it, but this is huge."

Excitedly, she grabbed my hand and dragged me into my room to change. "You are coming with me tonight, I might need you."

Her SUV bounded along the rural dirt roads until we arrived at the small home a few miles outside of town. It was quiet, with the lights turned low. A petite blond woman named Frances greeted us at the door. She hugged my mother warmly, then turned to me wide eyed. I could tell she recognized me, but she didn't approach me with the same familiarity. Readdressing my mother, her tone was dripping with concern.

"We have a stubborn one here, he's presenting breech and refusing to turn. I've already tried sifting with a rebozo and we are looking at a standing birth."

My mother looked to me and offered an introduction.

"Frances, this is my daughter Stella. Stella, this is one of our midwives, Frances. She truly is gifted in what she does. I am merely here in case she needs assistance."

Frances smiled and quickly pulled me into a hug as I outstretched my hand. "I've heard so many wonderful things about you, Stella. It's nice to finally meet you!"

I hugged back, and was interrupted by a woman howling in pain. Immediately, I ran to her side and dropped to my knees. She stopped and looked spooked at my uninvited presence. Her husband was seated behind her as she was bent down on her hands and knees, breathing through the contractions. She was panting heavily, and clearly in distress. Frances and my mother both stood in the doorway, choosing not to intervene. The couple looked to them, and they offered reassurance. The experience could only be described as autopilot. Without any recollection of how I had the knowledge, a deep part of me responded without effort.

"Let's drop your head toward the floor and rest on your elbows. I have an idea so we can try and get this little guy to turn, okay?"

Once again, they looked to those in the doorway and received confirmation to follow my direction.

"I need a few bags of frozen vegetables, please."

Stifling a laugh, the women ran to the fridge to get my requested items. Feeling a bit of relief from the changed position, the mother, whose name I later learned was Jenny, raised a brow. "What'd need with frozen peas? I ain't hungry, darling."

Her southern twang was sweet, with a touch of sarcasm. Her husband Dale rubbed her shoulders as she rocked back and forth, not even questioning what was taking place. Frances returned with the large plastic bowl of frozen bags. I grabbed one off the top, tossed it to Dale, and instructed him to help me hold them against her upper torso where the baby's head was.

"Babies do not like the cold, so we are going to use

these to encourage him to where he needs to be. Once he flips, we will get you in the pool to finish laboring, okay?"

"Whatever works, just get him out safely!"

Jenny's breathing increased as the contractions grew closer. I turned to Frances and asked how she was progressing.

"Five centimeters. That was an hour ago. You get that baby flipped and she will most likely go pretty shortly after."

My mother and Frances had their arms wrapped around each other as they watched me move synergistically with the family. A large blue tub with a plastic sheet covering it rested in the corner. Once I felt the baby start to move, a resounding burst of joy rippled through my body. I cheered, "Come on, baby! You can do it! You're almost here, move for your mama!"

Every one shouted together in an attempt to entice the little one into changing direction. We guided Jenny's head a little closer to the floor, and successfully encouraged the baby to turn. Immediately, Frances and my mother guided Jenny into the pool of water for the delivery. With adrenaline pumping, I raced out of the house and gripped the wood railing. More screaming and shouts of encouragement drifted through the home, pounding in my ears. A low bellowing noise hit my gut and I knew it was happening . . . a baby was being born.

With closed eyes, I dropped to the ground and began to weep. It was so beautiful and heartbreaking in the same breath. I wanted to scream as something new was rushing out of me. I could feel her inside, the woman I had become, whose body I inhabited. She was angry and bitter, fighting to the surface, but I had to fight back. The moon was full, lighting up the surroundings in a pale grey. At the bottom of the hill ran a small creek, iridescent with moonbeams bouncing off the surface. I knew I needed to calm down, or risk a debilitating headache. I walked quietly to the creek, dipped my hands into the cool water, and let it flow across my fingertips. Then I splashed my face a few times. The babbling brook soothed my nerves and slowed my heart rate.

I did not hear my mother walking toward me, it was only after she gently tapped my shoulder that I knew she was there.

"I think you are ready to know a little more about who you are. Let's go make some tea. It's going to be a long night."

I took her outstretched hand and leaned into her shoulder as we said our goodbyes to the others and walked back to her truck. I could not contain the tears once my eyes fell upon the baby happily nursing at his mother's breast. Jenny and Dale both looked to me and smiled with gratitude.

Frances walked out with us and opened the door for me. "Welcome back, Stella. We missed you."

I grinned back at her and offered a warm hug before climbing in. Trying to process everything that happened in just a few hours, the questions formed a list so long I was unsure where to begin. What kind of woman knows how to deliver babies, yet is covered with tattoos? I thought I was a singer. When did I leave? Why did I leave?

My mother was quiet as she rummaged through the cupboards for her tea strainers and coffee mugs. A kettle shrilled on the gas stove top for a moment, before she poured the steaming water over the herbs.

Holding the piping hot mug in my hands, I breathed the lemon and ginger aroma in before adding a few delicate cubes of sugar.

"Does everyone here know me?" I queried softly.

She took a sip of her tea while tapping her foot against the stool in the kitchen nervously. "Yes, they do. You lived here until you went away to college. You made many friends and adjusted well once you gave everyone a chance. Working with me also helped because you were able to get to know folks a lot faster. Initially, you were angry about what you lost, but you found ways to get along before the school year started."

I grinned knowing that I was happy here. She said I had made a lot of friends, so I questioned if any of them were around still, as I had not talked to anyone outside of the hospital before tonight and was quite lonely.

Her face dropped as she looked away. "Stella, honey, you stopped talking to people a while back. When you left, you vanished without a trace. If people see you and are somewhat surprised, it's not just because of the star you became, it's because of the person you were when you were here. No one ever expected you to see you again, myself included."

"Oh . . . do you know why?" I asked quietly.

My mother shook her head and shrugged. "No one knows, Stella. We knew you weren't taken, because you left a note in your apartment. You just said, "I can't do this anymore, don't look for me, it's best to let me go. I love you." We looked of course, but since you took off of free will and packed a suitcase, the police weren't too keen on doing a whole lot. When you made it big, we tried to see you, but you were gone."

Her heart had been annihilated in my absence. I stood up and pulled her tight into my arms. For so long, she had waited for her own questions to be answered. Unfortunately, I was unable to do so. The mystery of my departure weighed heavy in the room, and I couldn't take any more for the evening.

"It's probably best we don't know, mama. I can't imagine what would have happened to make me do something like that. I just thought I would ask. I'm getting really tired, but I have one more question if that's alright. What did I go to school for? Obviously, it was not what I became." I held out my arms, twisted them, and laughed at the ink I had grown to know so well.

My mother began to glow before answering. "Honey, you were in Pre-Med. You earned a full scholarship to UNC Chapel Hill. You were close enough to home, but it kept you so busy we didn't see you often. We were so proud of you, you did so well there."

We both sipped our tea solemnly for a bit. She was allowing me to absorb the information, and formulate new questions. It helped explain a little more about how I knew what to do tonight.

"Everything is past tense. Maybe someday I can make you proud again, because I have this feeling it's not something I did a lot of before the accident. I am not ready to know who she was, but I feel her. She lives in my bones, like a ghost haunting a house. Unwelcome, but thinks she belongs here. I suppose it makes sense, she doesn't have anywhere else to go. After all, I'm the ghost." I stood from the island in the kitchen and placed my mug into the sink before turning around and hugging my mother once more.

She held me close and rubbed my back. "Baby girl, you

are no ghost, this is who you were before the world failed you and your heart became stone. I never would have wished that this is what it would take to bring you back to me, but I won't deny the good Lord has blessed me each day you have been here. I've waited so long just to see your sweet face, and tell you that I love you."

Breaking the embrace, I stood back and held onto her hands, shaking. If I was such a cold person and all it would do was rip me away, I wasn't sure I wanted my memory back.

"Mama, if I go to sleep tonight and she's here when I wake up, know I am so sorry. I hope she knows that you love her, and whatever happened to her wasn't her fault. I know people blame God, or their parents—things outside of themselves for what's wrong in life. But if she comes back, she needs to know she has a choice. She can keep being the person she was, or she can become the person she was always meant to be. Hopefully it will be me, but with all of the memories. If I ended up being as smart as you tell me I was, her heart must have been broken pretty bad to shut everyone and everything out. And if it's just me that wakes up in the morning, please don't tell me anymore. Can you do that?"

Wiping away the tears, she nodded profusely. "Of course, Honey. I won't tell you anything you don't ask."

She kissed me goodnight, and I headed to my room. As I walked down the hall, I saw my father in the den watching a football game. He had been very reserved since I came home, nothing like I remembered him being. His emotional absence was the hardest thing to overcome. I stood in the doorway and waited for him to invite me in, which he did after muting the game.

Sitting on the opposite couch, I said the only thing I

could, "Daddy, I don't know what I did to hurt you so you bad, other than taking off, which I know must have been so hard on you. I don't want to know. I told mama the same thing. I know it's not as easy for you to look past things as it is for her. Whatever happened, I hope you can find it in your heart to forgive me."

He said nothing for a few moments, making me believe I was being dismissed, but as I leaned my arm over to stand, he motioned for me to sit down. "Stella, I should apologize to you. At the very least explain my feelings. I heard you and your mama having your heart to heart, so I know there's a lot of emotion right now. My feelings have nothing to do with forgiving you. Hell, I know you can't recall a thing past seventeen, and that must be scary. But when you left here, you took your mama's heart with you. Things were real rough for a while. I even thought we weren't going to make it. But we did, and no matter how hard I try, I don't know what I will do if your memory comes back and you take off again. Your mama is thrilled to have you here, as am I. But I have to protect her, because we all know there are no guarantees. I understand you not wanting to know, and for now that's okay. But just because you don't remember, doesn't mean we have forgotten. You aren't the only one struggling here, and the truth will come out."

The conversation solidified my view that my mother was overcompensating with affection. Rather than being wounded by his words, he merely confirmed what I already knew. Before walking out of the room, I held the doorpost for support, as my legs were still a bit unsteady.

"Daddy, you and I aren't that different, you know. We're both afraid of the same thing."

I didn't wait for his response. I wanted nothing more

than to crawl into my bed and sleep. An exhaustion I had not known before came over me as my body rested under the heavy quilts. There were no dreams; I had stopped having them, or I simply could not remember them. When I closed my eyes, I knew for certain what would stay the same—nothing.

Chapter 4

~ The Sun Will Rise ~

I woke up long before dawn, an uncontrollable restlessness overcame me. I took great care not to wake anyone, including our pit bull, Zoey. She slept soundly at the foot of my bed, only lifting her head for a moment when I slipped on my shoes and left the house. For the first time since I arrived, I dared to venture out on my own. The town was small, and not likely to place me in any danger. Green-hued lights emanated from the street lamps making the dirt road leading into town a bit more visible. Crickets and frogs sang as I walked slowly toward the small brick buildings.

The older shops still held those open glass windows, where they elaborately decorated the displays. I passed a shoe store, an appliance repair facility, and hardware store before my nose caught the delicate scent of fresh breads baking. My mother told me there was a French bakery in town that I had always loved. Once a week, she would bring back crusty loaves of bread and delicious pastries that I would devour almost immediately. I favored a tiny lemon tart with powdered sugar and candied citrus peels sprinkled on top. The chocolates were often too sweet, but I tried them anyway.

Around the corner, I spied the old metal sign hanging out from the doorway. It was a whimsical building, with flowers spilling out from hanging window containers. Small iron tables were scattered on the brick patio, with chairs tilted against the edge for easy sweeping. Curious about the place, I crept closer to the shop and peeked into the windows as the workers busied themselves for the day. My mouth watered as I watched trays of desserts being set out with care in the display cases, and baskets on racks filled with steaming breads of all kinds. I pressed my hand to the cool glass for a moment to steady my legs, when I felt a tap on my shoulder. Startled, I grabbed the wall to keep from falling, and the man reached out to hold me in place.

He could tell I was frightened and stepped back a bit. "We open in an hour. But if you see something you want, I can get it for you. My treat."

Unable to speak, I simply shook my head and slid against the wall, moving away from the bakery and the stranger.

I rubbed my hand across my head nervously, and realized I forgot to wear a scarf. There was nothing to cover my ugly scars, not even the hair that had grown out a bit. Embarrassed, my chin dropped low. "No thank you."

I was mortified beyond belief. Not only was he kind, he was beautiful. Even in the dark, under the brim of his ball cap, I could tell his eyes were intense and captivating. Long lashes brushed his strong cheek bones in the brief moments he blinked. Patches of flour that transferred off his clothing dusted the black hooded jacket I was wearing, and the top of my head came just shy of his chin, which I noticed during the two seconds I had curved perfectly into his body.

We were at a standstill; I was too afraid to move, but wanted to run. It was so quiet I could hear every labored breath coming from his chest. It was the ringing of the door from inside of the bakery that broke the awkwardness between us.

"Hey, Julian, when you go to the store today, we need more baking soda. We have enough right now, but it's. . . ." The man was loud until he noticed something was distracting the person he was speaking to. It was the break I needed to run, and for the first time since the accident, I did just that.

I could hear him yell at me to stop, but he did not chase after me. I ran past the hardware store, clear to the edge of town. It wasn't that much of a distance, but to someone who had spent weeks learning to walk again, it gave hope. I held onto the metal street lamp, sat against the base, and cried. Not out of despair, but relief. I grabbed my knees and kissed them repeatedly, thankful for their strength and the physical therapist that pushed me to always try harder.

The imprints of white fingertips on my shoulders brought just as much excitement. It was my first encounter with someone that made my heart flutter, and I knew his name. Julian. *Julian. Julian.* I said it over and over again, just to hear the way it poured off my tongue and caressed my lips. I knew I would never stand a chance with someone like him, especially now, but it did not keep my heart from pounding and consuming every thought. I crept back into the house. Everyone was still asleep, and would be none the wiser to my morning adventure. Settling back into bed, Zoey crawled under the sheets and warmed my chilled limbs, as the thought of Julian heated my blood.

While I finally found rest, my mother opened my bedroom door to announce she was leaving. Her patient, Raina Moreau, was having a difficult day and faced the possibility of being admitted to the hospital. Her white cell counts were really off, which was not a good sign.

"I am going to draw some blood samples. Stella, you can come with me if you want, but I thought you might enjoy the rest. I know you do not sleep well, so I am sorry to wake you, but I didn't want you to be worried."

Her hand brushed across my forehead and lingered over the scars, thick with hardened tissue and bumps from the staples. I turned away from her touch, remembering how his eyes traveled over the same places.

Softly, she reached back up and touched my cheek. "They are a testament to your will, do not be ashamed. In another month or so, no one will even notice."

"I know, mom. They just bother me. I don't feel pretty as it is, and those just add to it. I feel like a monster. Not just because of those, but the tattoos, everything. These are forever, they aren't going away." I held my arms out. I had come to appreciate the artwork, but this wasn't the body I knew. If I knew what was behind them, I might have appreciated them more. I wavered between acceptance and denial of my body almost hourly.

"You are no more a monster than I am the Queen of England, so hush. When I get back, we are going to the farmers market. You need to get out of the house, so enjoy your nap."

I smiled and rubbed my mother's hand, which rested on my shoulder.

"Yes, mama. Real quick, though, what's going on with Mrs. Moreau? I hear you talk about her all the time. You're obviously very close, but I don't know what's wrong with her."

She held back her tears, but I could see my question drew a sadness from deep within her. "Raina is my best friend, and she has Stage three breast cancer. She's had the mastectomy, and even several lymph nodes removed, but it was so aggressive when we found it, there was little that could be done. She has lesions on her brain that interfere with her ability to walk. She can barely eat, and is on painkillers most of the time because of the chemotherapy. I have gotten more time with her than I thought I would, but now it's just a matter of waiting for the day to finally come."

The distress my mother was experiencing was more than I could bear. I pulled her into my arms and held tight as she let herself go. Knowing now what she was enduring, in addition to taking care of me, forced any self-pity I was wallowing in to leave immediately. Her heart was in the blender, and life was pressing the power button. As a physician, she developed a certain sort of detachment, which was professionally necessary. But this wasn't work. This was her best friend and child under her wings, and she was damn sure to do everything in her power to make the best of it, despite knowing that for all the skill and knowledge she possessed, ultimately life and death was not dependent on her, but on the unseen forces of the almighty and his will.

Chapter 5

~ Intervention ~

My mother returned from Mrs. Moreau's in high spirits. She said they did not have to admit her today. Somehow things were more stable and she was feeling better. In more ways than one, it was a good day for us both. I had showered and slipped into a soft cotton sundress with a mid-sleeve cardigan. Although it did not fully cover my arms, it was far too warm and the ink was not going anywhere. The top drawer of the dresser held a stack of bandannas my mother had sewn for me to cover my head. They looked cute with the tiny corners of hair peeking out from above my ears and around my neckline. A costume pair of horn-rimmed sunglasses was in a box labeled "Halloween," along with a strand of faux pearls. There was also a felt poodle skirt in the box, which I passed over without question. However, the rest tied into a retro chic look, as my mother called it.

As we were preparing to leave, she approached me with a small metal tube and twisted the lid off. "Pout your lips, Stella."

I followed her direction and puckered them into the fish-like shape one makes when applying lipstick. As she pulled her hand away, I noticed she was holding a vibrant red hue.

"Go look, it's perfect."

Hesitantly, I walked into the bathroom to look at myself in the mirror. While barely touching the crimson stain on my full lips, I was in awe for the first time at the face looking back. It wasn't the girl I thought I was, or the monster whose body I held captive. It was a normal person, about to enjoy a day at the market. My scars were hidden, and thoughts of Julian brought a slight flush to my cheeks. If he were to see me like this, surely I would not be so afraid. Knowing he was most likely still at the bakery, my stomach dropped slightly.

"Let's go, Stella. We only have a little longer before the vendors leave. I want to make a nice dinner for us."

With one last glance, I smiled and pulled down my shades while closing the door.

The sun was bright and delicious against my skin, as we walked down the road into town holding baskets and produce nets. I listened to my mother ramble on about nothing, and enjoyed the slight breeze flowing through the surrounding trees. This town was beautiful, and I had barely seen any of it yet. It was the first farmers market of the season, so everyone in town was anxious to get out and socialize. I trusted my mom not to put me in a situation that I couldn't handle, so I stayed close and smiled as she talked to everyone she passed.

I found myself doing most of the shopping, while she chattered about. I took the time to smell the crisp fruits and taste the fresh cheeses, and every bite was an awakening of the senses. I scarcely heard the world around me, completely focused on each stop. She would grab my arm occasionally and turn me around to shake someone's hand, before they went right back into the conversation.

While I was trying a sample of homemade cinnamon apple butter, my mother grabbed my arm and squealed, "Oh, Stella . . . try this tart, its divine!" She groaned unnecessarily as she reached over to put the half-eaten piece into my mouth.

Within a few bites, my eyes closed and made the same exaggerated noises.

"I told you that you could have had anything you wanted. I'm glad you came back for it."

Frozen, I opened my eyes to an equally-shocked expression on my mother's face. She looked past me with a half grin, half-questioning look. I turned slowly to come eye to eye once again with a man who made me feel things I had never felt before, at least not that I remembered. In the light, I could see his eyes were the most beautiful shade of green. A rough shadow of growth covered his chin and neck, trailing down onto his Adam's apple. The muscles of his shoulders and chest pushed against the snug sheer cotton T-shirt he wore with a black striped apron and distressed grey ball cap. Without realizing it, I ran my fingers along the surface of the bandana. When I felt the prickly strands poking through the fabric, I looked away embarrassed. I looked back to my mother, who had silently watched the interaction take place.

"You know each other?" she voiced suspiciously.

Julian laughed and walked over to give my mother a big hug, causing my jaw to drop. "No, Sandy, not yet. We met briefly this morning when she was outside of the shop. I tried to say hi, but I think I scared her," he said with a chuckle.

"You were at the shop this morning?"

She walked closer to me, causing my flight instincts to rise again. "I couldn't sleep, so I went for a walk. I smelled the bread. It was nice. That's all."

My mother laughed so heartily, I thought she had lost her mind. She walked back over to Julian and slid her arm familiarly around his waist. Patting his chest lightly, she offered an introduction. "Julian, this is my daughter, Stella. Stella, this is Julian. Raina is his mother. He came back from New York when she was unable to take care of things any longer. This makes it . . . two years now?"

He smiled at my mother and squeezed back. It was indisputable the affection they held for one another. I wanted to be jealous of this stranger, but it was hard to hate someone so handsome. He reached out his hand in my direction.

I took it lightly and shook back. "Nice to meet you again, Julian. I am sorry I took off like that. I get . . ."My lip worried between my teeth, trying to find the right words.

He came to my rescue and put his hand up in the air. "No need to explain, Stella. I am a stranger, after all. Hopefully that will change now."

Appreciative of his kindness, I grinned while thinking about how much I would like that. My mother was practically ready to burst standing next to him as she held up our baskets.

"Julian, you have to come to dinner tonight! It's been

so long and I know you need the break. She will be okay. You know she worries about you working so hard. Please say yes. Besides, Jim will be thrilled to have another guy over to talk shop."

Knowing that my mother was referring to his mother made me sad for Julian. Two years taking care of a parent and running the family business. I wondered what he had done in New York. I wondered if I knew him when I was younger.

After he agreed happily to the invitation, I was determined to find out if we were acquaintances. "Julian, how old are you?" I wondered aloud.

"Thirty four," he replied. "Why do you ask?"

I shrugged my shoulders and took a basket from my mother. "I was just wondering if we knew each other, and you were just being nice because you know I don't remember anything. Because I know for a fact that you know who I am."

My mother looked guilty and peered up at Julian.

His expression was flat and unreadable. After a few moments of awkward silence, he smiled and shifted his hat. "I know who you were, but I don't know who you are now. It's a blank slate for both of us, don't you think?"

Happy with that answer, I nodded my head. "See you tonight, Julian."

"See you, Stella."

As we walked away, my mother bumped my shoulder. "You have some explaining to do, missy! Why didn't you tell me you went into town this morning? It must have been before dawn."

"It was. I couldn't sleep, like always. I have been good

on my feet for a bit, so I thought I would take a walk. Mama, I ran. I really ran. And it felt so good!"

She laughed loudly again. "Yeah, you were running away from a man. I never thought that would be the thing to test your legs."

Playfully bumping her again, I felt the need to ask more questions before dinner. "Julian said he knew me. How did we meet, do you know?"

Her tone became more serious with the question. "You met him at school. He just turned thirty-four, so you are not too far apart in age, just a few months. Shortly after graduation, he joined the Navy and was deployed to Afghanistan. You used to write him letters and make care packages for him."

"So we were friends!" I said excitedly, and then remembered what she said earlier about leaving town without a thought. "He's another person who never heard from me again, isn't he."

Nodding her head, she said nothing the rest of the way home. Feeling the mood sour, I stopped her from opening the door. "He said it's a blank slate for both of us. Let us keep it that way, okay? Tonight will be a good night. I am going to help you make dinner."

My words made her drop her basket and give me a strong embrace. I held her back tightly. I found something that made my mother happy, and consequently, was making me happy. If giving Julian a chance meant giving my mom so much joy, I would be happy to, and I would gladly move heaven and earth to keep it that way.

After hearing that Julian would be joining us for dinner, even my father's mood grew more buoyant. He placed the radio on a jazz station and danced with my mother in the kitchen while we cooked. The tomatoes simmered with the fresh herbs, while pasta boiled next to it. My mother took the large slotted spoon from my hand and stirred, while giving my father a look. His hand extended to mine and pulled me close for a dance. I remembered that when I was a little girl he would have me stand on his feet while he shuffled back and forth slowly to the music. I would cling to the back of his thighs with my little arms as mom swayed behind him. As a family, we moved in a soft rhythm.

Tears welled up and soaked his shirt as the music played. I felt his chest jerk under my cheeks, then my mother came up behind us and held on as we shifted in circles. We danced until the song ended, and laughed once we lifted our heads and wiped the tears away. The doorbell rang, interrupting the dance and drawing my attention. Butterflies collided in my gut knowing who was on the porch. On the other side of the screen door, Julian stood, looking nervous, and wearing a brick red shirt with a pair of worn jeans. In his arms rested a large paper-wrapped bouquet of gladiolus. He looked at my tattoos and smiled brightly while handing them to me.

"I know they are your favorite, I hope you don't mind."

I smiled broadly, while allowing the petals to tickle my nose. "They are beautiful, thank you. Please come in."

When I opened the door, Julian passed by me into the foyer, and then walked into the kitchen where my parents greeted him with hugs. A small bag hung from his arm, with a brown cardboard box inside. He pulled it out and handed it over to my mother, who peeked inside immediately and shrieked.

"Sandy, that's dessert. She insisted."

Julian playfully chastised my mother, while my dad patted his back with the same fondness my mother held. "I hear Raina is having a good day, Julian. It's been a while since we've had you over. Like old times, eh?"

While I watched in the doorway, the scene became overwhelming. The monster within reminded me I was merely a bystander to a life that was not mine. I set the flowers down on the sofa and walked onto the front porch, then sat in the swing and pushed off aggressively with my tiptoes. The citronella candles gave a sweet aroma to the cool air. Although the mosquitoes were not out yet, my mother had insisted on lighting them for ambiance. I heard the screen door creak open, and wished for nothing more than to be left alone.

Julian came around to the front of the swing and leaned against the wooden rail. "Mind if I join you?" he asked softly.

Simply nodding my head, I looked off into the distance. I hated feeling the way I did, but I was unable to control it. He moved slowly and sat next to me, without saying anything at first. We watched the sunset, listening to the sounds of night beginning its serenade.

Once darkness gave way to the starlit sky, he turned to me and said, "What's wrong, Stella?"

"What makes you think there is something wrong?" I replied shortly. I didn't need to ask, because my distress was palpable.

"Do you want me to leave? If I make you uncomfortable, I will."

Shaking my head, I rubbed my hands together nervously.

"No, you make my parents happy. Everything makes me uncomfortable, I just need to get used to it. If I could leave, I would, but I have nowhere to go." My voice was barely a whisper. Shaking from the cold, my teeth began to chatter. I tried to hide it, but he noticed and told me to wait as he retrieved a blanket from inside. He pulled it around us, wrapped his arm around me, and rubbed my shoulder briskly to warm me up.

"Now where were we? Oh yes. What's bothering Stella?"

The smell of him so near and the warmth of his body caused any animosity I'd had toward him to vanish. If we'd been friends in the past, it was clear he still cared about me, because he could read me so well. Even my own mother was unable to decipher my moods from time to time.

"It's hard to explain. I feel like I am living a time warp. In my head I know that this is my real body, but in my heart I am someone else. Whoever I became was so unhappy. Every day I feel her inside, just waiting to come out, and I am scared to death of the day that happens. My mom told me that you and I used to be friends. But she also told me that I disappeared one day, which makes you one more person I hurt, and I have no way of fixing it. So forgive me if I am distant, I'm just trying to prevent something bad from happening."

Julian's arms tightened around me. "Stella, do you really feel that you are responsible for the things you don't remember?"

"In a way I do. It's like my dad told me last night; I might not remember, but you haven't forgotten. I am just protecting people. It's easier to stay away until my memory comes back. And then no one will have to worry about me." I tried to hold in the sobs, but they choked out in tiny bursts.

"Your dad told you that last night?"

Nodding my head, I wiped my nose to keep it from running onto Julian's shirt. His breathing increased, and he appeared to grow angry.

"Julian, he's right. It's okay. He's just watching out for my mom. I get that no one knows what happened to me, and what little they did know, I told them not to tell me. Just like with you, whatever I did to you, please don't tell me, because I am unable to atone for it. And if and when my memory comes back, just know in this moment, I am so very sorry."

Julian's hand came up to my cheek and wiped away the tears as they fell toward my chin. I sniffled, then laughed and wiped my nose against my arm again.

"Stella, I was never angry at you. Hurt? Absolutely, I was devastated. I won't tell you why, but I will tell you this—we were not just friends, you were my best friend, and I have missed you so much. When I saw you this morning, it took everything in me not to pull you into my arms. I didn't want to frighten you. I knew you were scared, and that's why I didn't follow you."

I tried to smile, but could not stop the tremble in my lips. It was no wonder he made me feel so many different things. He knew me better than I knew myself.

"I'm still sorry, Julian," I uttered while more tears fell over his hand, which remained pressed against my cheeks. He pulled me close, and my face rested upon his chest where I could hear his heart pounding furiously.

"I still love you, Stella," he said.

Chapter 6

~ Spark ~

Julian's revelation sent electricity through my veins, down to the very tips of my fingers and toes. *I still love you.*

I swallowed back hard, and then jumped after the screen door creaked open, my mother stopping at the threshold. "Well, aren't you two cozy. Supper is on the table and your father is starting to howl with hunger pangs. Best you get in here before there is nothing left."

Julian held me in place while glancing over his shoulder and responding. "We will be right in, Sandy."

She smiled at us both before gently closing the door. Turning toward Julian with my head lowered, I breathed deeply to settle my palpitating heart.

"I shouldn't have said that, Stella. I'm sorry. It's just . . . this is hard for me."

I worried my lip out of concern, and started to get restless. I slipped the blanket off my shoulders, then stood and turned around, reaching my hand out with a grin. "It's just spaghetti. I think we can manage."

Julian's face broke into a beautiful smile. He took my hand in his, and pulled me into the same familiar embrace from earlier in the morning. I buried my nose into the corner of his neck, and closed my eyes while inhaling his scent. A spark ignited in my brain, causing my body to jerk for a split second. Embarrassed, I tried to pull away.

"Stella, what just happened?" he asked with concern.

Avoiding his stare, I could feel the tears fighting to the surface. He used his hand to gently bring my chin upward, and the pad of his thumbs stroked my cheeks softly to wipe the dampness away.

Shaking my head, I took a step back. "I don't know. I just smelled you, and there was this flash. It was so fast."

Julian took a firm step backward, and placed his hands behind his neck while looking at me in deep thought. Several awkward moments passed before he seemed to resolve whatever conflict was raging in his own mind. "Stella, I want you to smell me again. I know it sounds weird, but please, just try it. I think it's important."

I looked at Julian hesitantly. He kept his posture rigid, and was completely serious. I stepped toward him slowly, then gently placed my fingers on his ribs and leaned closer. He held his own breath as mine gently swept across his neck. Inhaling deeply, I felt more relaxed, but the spark was gone. Disappointed and unsure of what was to be expected, I lowered down onto my heels and stepped back. The look on my face told him that whatever he was hoping would happen, did not. He placed his hand on my lower back, and guided me into the house.

With a hushed voice, he eased my anxious thoughts. "Some things take time. There is no need to rush. I think

I know what happened, but we can talk about it later. It's a good sign."

I turned and smiled while entering the dining room. Sandy had already opened a bottle of wine and was laughing with my father, whom Julian sat next to after pulling out my chair. The music played softly in the background, as my family home felt full of life. Everyone seemed at peace in the moment, even me. Throughout the dinner, I couldn't stop looking at Julian, taking in his every feature and nuance. The way his bone structure was strong and sharp, and how his eyes were constantly moving about in assessment, breaking everything down in his mind, despite his leisurely demeanor. My gaze fell to his lips, but did not remain very long before my wanderings were interrupted.

"Stella, stop it. It's rude to stare at people," my father said, admonishing me sternly.

Immediately, the air was pulled out of my lungs at the childish scolding. I clenched my jaw to keep from getting upset, and lowered my eyes to my plate while pushing the last bites around. My appetite had vanished, and I wanted nothing more than to disappear.

"I am sorry, Julian," I said quietly.

The mood of dinner had changed, and suddenly grew quiet. I wanted nothing more than to see his face again, but dared not take another glance.

"Stella, look at me," Julian said gently.

I refused, and the tears welled up in my eyes. I hated this feeling.

He then repeated himself with more authority. "Stella, look at me."

I slowly raised my head, and our eyes met as the tears poured down. I looked over to my father, and his face was full of resentment at being challenged in his own home. I turned my head, pushed my plate away, and requested to be excused. No one responded, so I started to scoot my chair back.

Before I could rise, Julian brought his fist to his mouth and coughed to gain attention.

"You know, Stella, your memories are tied to your senses. The way things taste, sound, feel, smell, and look. At any given time, a particular stimulus can trigger them. If looking at me helps you to remember something, stare as long as you like. I don't mind."

He laughed to break the tension, but I could not stop the quiver in my chin. After choosing to ignore my father's sour behavior, I could see the look on my mother's face hoping for things to settle.

I scooted my seat back toward the table and chose to sate my curiosity. "So, Julian, how is it you happen to know so much about memories?"

His face became a bit more serious, and he looked to my parents before coming back to me. "Back in New York, I did a lot of work at the VA hospital with soldier's returning from war. My time in Afghanistan really opened my eyes, and I saw a lot of good men break down from mental health issues, especially post-traumatic stress disorder. Unless you have been there, it's really hard to understand. I convinced the mental health staff to adopt more holistic practices, in addition to the medications. I guess you could say Sandy had a bigger impact on me growing up than I realized."

I looked over to my mom, and her face was beaming

with pride. The connection made more sense than her just caring for his ailing mother, and it also raised more questions about Julian.

"What exactly did you do in the Navy?"

Julian looked over to my mother, as if unsure about disclosing his position. Her face could not have been any brighter.

Gauging his hesitation, she answered for him. "He is a doctor, Stella. A psychiatrist, and a damn good one."

My mother's use of a curse word caused me to pause. I understood why Julian might be hesitant to tell me what he did. Thoughts swarmed my brain about the strange encounter. What were the odds I would run into, or should I say away from, someone who might actually understand where I am and what I am going through. Suddenly, his intense gaze was no longer magnetic, but intimidating. He wasn't attracted to me, he was analyzing me. He knew who I was, and wanted to help my mother. My heart felt like it was going to beat out of my chest as my skin grew tight and uncomfortable. I wanted out of my chair, the house . . . my very body. The confused stares of those around the table only amplified the terror that was starting to grow within.

"I . . . I . . . I need to go on a walk. I am sorry. Excuse me," I choked out. I bolted from my chair and heard the others clamoring after me, but I refused to turn around. I just wanted to run as far away as I could. Tears clouded my vision as my feet struggled not to slip on the gravel road. Julian was not far behind, as I could hear the crunching rocks beneath his feet. He did not call out or try to stop me. From a distance, he kept my pace and allowed me to exhaust all of my energy. When I finally stopped and was panting heavily, Julian's face was full of genuine concern. He still said nothing, and waited for me to speak first.

"Well, doctor, aren't you going to say anything?" I asked sarcastically.

"Stella, stop. I am not here to treat you."

"Then what are you doing here?"

"I already told you. You were my best friend. Do I want to help you? Absolutely, but only if you want me to. You are not my patient. I would never cross that line without being invited. There has to be a level of trust, which is earned."

He was right in knowing I did not trust him. I wanted to more than anything, and felt like I could. But if nothing else, I have learned feelings are wild and uncontrollable demons. If only he could help me to control those, there might be hope for me.

"Did my mother ask if you would treat me?"

Julian wrestled once again with telling me the truth, carefully formulating the words in his head, but deciding to be honest. "Yes, she did. But I told her no."

We began walking back slowly to the house, allowing long moments to pass between us. Crickets continued the evening serenade, along with the frogs and other creatures of the night. It was dark, with only the porch light off in the distance. The moon was casting a low glow on the dirt road, contrasting the small pebbles against the roadside brush.

"Why did you tell her no, Julian? If you thought you could help me, and you wanted to, what stopped you?" I wasn't sure I truly wanted to know the answer, but there was nothing to lose. I had been avoiding so many questions, but I deemed this one necessary, as it dealt not with the past, but the present.

He exhaled heavily and slowed down a bit more. "I am not really in a place mentally to be guiding other people. It takes a lot out of you to break down those barriers. It is very rewarding work, but you have to be able to separate yourself from it to make the best decisions. With you, it would be personal. Professional objectivity is important for any physician, so the practice is largely discouraged. Look at your own mom as an example. For the most part, others have treated you. Sandy oversees the care of course, but often personal feelings have interfered, and she was forced to take a step back."

I nodded in understanding and stopped on the first step of the porch, then turned around and placed my hands on Julian's shoulders. I did not know him, but I could feel the weight he carried. He was incredibly stoic, but I sensed he was tired.

"Julian, who is taking care of you?" I asked quietly.

The muscles in his arms tensed beneath my palms and he swallowed hard. He turned his head and breathed out, then he brought his gaze back to mine. "Nobody takes care of me, Stella," he said solemnly.

I released my own breath and stepped back off of the porch, while looking Julian square in the eyes. In just one day, he had surprised me several times over. Without asking, I reached my arms around his waist and squeezed tightly. His arms folded softly over mine as he tucked his nose into the crook of my neck.

"Well thank you for taking care of me today, Julian. It means a lot."

He squeezed a bit tighter and let go, then he stepped

back and looked up to the house. "I have to go, do you mind telling your folks goodbye and thank you for dinner?"

Nodding, I replied, "Yeah, of course. Will I see you again?"

His mouth cracked into one of those dizzying smiles. "Do you want to see me again?"

I rolled my eyes and laughed lightly. "I wouldn't have asked if I didn't, silly."

Julian took a step forward, so close I could smell the soap and sweat clinging to his shirt. "How about coming by the bakery tomorrow, and actually coming inside."

I curled my nose at his sarcastic humor, then blushed. The magnetic force of his stare returned and caused my heart rate to speed up. "Tomorrow it is," I whispered.

"See ya." He smiled back.

Walking to his truck, he had a little skip to his step. The flutters in my stomach were just as nerve wracking as the fifty other emotions that barreled through me at any given time. I would take those over the sinking feeling any day. He waved before turning onto the dark road, and I watched as the red tail lights disappeared.

I failed to realize my mother had been sitting on the front porch the whole time we were there, hidden beneath the porch light out of view.

"Momma, you startled me!" I laughed.

She patted the seat next to her, inviting me to sit. "Stella, are you okay now?" she asked with worry in her voice.

"Yes, I am sorry I ran off. I don't know what came

over me."

"It's okay, Stella. Julian seemed to know what to do. It's funny, I asked if he would take you on, and he told me no. Yet it appears he has somewhat changed his mind and is helping you."

I shook my head. "No mama, he didn't. He said it went against being a doctor. He wants to, but doesn't feel he should."

My mother wrapped her arm around me, and she pulled me closer into her side. I laid my head on her shoulder while our tip toes pushed the swing back and forth.

As her fingers gently grazed my scalp in a loving caress, she began to speak with equal affection. "Stella, helping someone is different than treating them. He is correct. You are not supposed to treat family and friends. As a physician, it is the most difficult thing for me to do when it comes to you and Raina. I want the very best, and even for all of the knowledge and resources I possess and have access to, my hands are tied when it comes to God's will. I cannot force your memory to come back any more than I can cause the cancer to leave Raina's body. I must stand by and hope that He is on my side, and the side of those who are in charge of your treatment. As for help, though, I can do that. So can Julian. Helping someone is picking up where medicine leaves off. It is where healing takes place, as well as the hurt. Your struggle is not just in your brain, but in your mind. They are two different things, and folks often forget that. The more people you have to help you through this, the better equipped you will be to cope with these changes, whatever they may be."

Although it was confusing, I knew what she meant. I had been so reluctant to be social, to allow anyone in. He was just one person. One person who happened to know me better than I knew myself. I pushed past the turmoil and forced myself for once to believe something good could actually come of this.

Chapter 7

~ Early Bird ~

Sleep did not come easily. For several hours, I tossed and turned with images of Julian flashing through my mind. I had crushes on boys growing up, but never dated anyone. I was too busy with the swim team and volunteering at the hospital to bother with investing in fleeting relationships. The fact my father was an Elder in the church didn't make it any easier. My friends all had boyfriends, but I was last for everything. I was the last to start my period, to get breasts, and to get my first kiss, which was terrible. I was so disappointed by the experience, that I had no interest in trying it again just for the sake of knowing something different. But I would kiss Julian. His lips were full and soft in appearance. I imagined he tasted like the lemon tart from the market, sweet but not overbearing. I struggled to recall the details of his face. The shadow of dark growth across his chin, and how his eyes looked almost black unless you stood closely and could see they were a stunning shade of evergreen. I was falling fast, and like with all of my other emotions, I had no idea how I would maintain control.

It seemed as though sharing them with Julian might be helpful, although the thought of not being well received was a hindrance. I really did not need to add rejection to my list of issues, so I buried the feelings deep and vowed to hide them as best I could. It was long before sunrise when I finally rolled out of bed and pulled on my sneakers and a light jacket. After kissing Zoey on the head, I crept out of the house and began the familiar walk into town. The smell of dew on the grass was strong in the morning air, and small animals scurried into the field as I approached. It did not take long to reach the edge of town and pass the light post that I rested on just twenty-four hours earlier. I navigated easily to the bakery and sat on the steps, arriving before Julian or any of the other workers. Only about five minutes went by before I became restless and started to take the chairs off of the tables and arrange them all around. An old wooden broom was perched in the corner, though the steps had clearly been swept the night before.

As I was opening up the patio umbrellas over the tables, Julian announced his arrival from a distance, presumably not to startle me.

"Wow, I wasn't expecting you so early. Have you been here a while?" he asked.

Scratching my head, I sheepishly nodded. "Yeah, I couldn't sleep so I decided to come over. I hope you don't mind. I can go home. I don't want to get in your way."

Julian smiled and walked up the steps with me behind him, then slid the key into the door and pulled it to twist the lock.

"Actually, I am really glad you are here. The manager

is sick and sent me a text last night saying she couldn't come in. It was just going to be Terry and I, which would have been a rough start to an already crappy day."

I followed him into the small shop, and my eyes scrutinized the display cases up close as he turned on the lights.

"Well, I don't know how helpful I will be, but I will try my best. Just tell me what to do, and hopefully I can make it better."

Julian walked into the kitchen and beckoned me to come with him. He lifted an apron from a hook and tossed it to me, before pulling pans and mixing bowls from shelves all around.

"We need to start the turnovers and doughnuts. Most people do not buy bread until later in the morning, and Terry will be here soon so he can start that. I am going to have you peel some apples, and I will roll out the dough. Does that sound okay?"

It seemed simple enough. For the next hour, I peeled nearly twenty pounds of apples and cut them into chunks, simmering them in a sugary concoction of cinnamon and syrup. Julian baked the turnovers without the apple mix, and piped it into the dough pockets after they came out of the oven and cooled slightly. He explained they stayed flakier that way, and let me try a few times to fill them. Unfortunately, I squeezed too hard and made a mess all over the counter. I learned how to use the mixer and managed to roll out and press the doughnuts, frying and flipping them to perfection. Some were glazed and sprinkled, others cream filled and dusted with powdered sugar. I couldn't believe that Julian was able to do all this at one time, but he had a routine, and I did my best not to disrupt the system. Terry showed up, and after a hasty introduction, had multiple loaves of delicious-smelling bread baking in the oven in no time.

The guys joked about a bonfire that Terry had attended the evening before. He insisted it was over twenty feet tall and just as wide, taking pride in solely igniting the inferno. I asked if there were marshmallow s'mores, but he said no.

I shook my head and went back to dusting doughnuts mumbling to myself, "What good is a fire with no marshmallows?"

Both of the men laughed as we got the bakery ready for business, with a few more employees straggling in throughout the morning. Julian did not seem like a very strict boss, but everyone worked very hard once they clocked in. The place was bustling with activity, and I spent my time restocking the displays and bussing the tables on the patio. The activity was somewhat tiring, but a welcome respite from hours at home alone. No one seemed to mind the bandanna covering my head, or gave me strange looks. For the first time since my arrival in North Carolina, I actually felt normal. The joy surged through my heart at the ease of interacting with others. I smiled, and so did they. Occasionally, I would turn to catch Julian watching me, but with contentment. The day passed too quickly, and before I knew it, Julian's shift was over and he was free for the afternoon. He had some shopping to do for the bakery, and asked if I wanted to join him.

I did not hesitate to jump into his truck and speed off into the city. Julian purchased the bulk of his supplies from a food warehouse in Charlotte. As we pushed the mammoth cart around and loaded it with cooking oils and flour, he began to ask how I felt about the day and what I liked best. I started to ramble on about several things before realizing it might be his way of assessing me. I assumed it was difficult to refrain from what you do naturally, but I didn't like feeling as though the experience was a test. Since he sensed my withdrawal, I told him exactly how I felt.

In the middle of the coffee aisle, he stopped the cart and exhaled deeply. "Stella, I told you that you were not my patient. I am not treating you. I just wanted to know if you enjoyed yourself. That is all."

I blushed with embarrassment and turned away. "I'm sorry."

"Stella, stop apologizing for how you feel. I want to know how you feel, as a friend. You should express your feelings, not hide them."

I laughed and traced my finger along the steel edge of the shopping cart. "Are you sure you are not trying to be a doctor right now?"

Julian's brows furrowed. "I will always be a doctor. It is who I am. I ask questions. But I am not *your* doctor."

I knew this could go back and forth infinitely. Taking the lead and answering the way he was requesting, I listed off every highlight of my day, which was pretty much every moment. Even peeling the chewed bubblegum from under the table ledges was not bothersome. We began to walk again, and finished pulling the necessary items. After loading the truck, I felt myself begin to grow tired. As much as I tried to keep myself awake, I felt my head bob back and forth multiple times as I drifted in and out of sleep. When I came to, I was tucked into my bed and night had fallen. The light was still on and my parents were speaking quietly in the kitchen.

I padded down the hall and into the dimly-lit room. Dinner had already been served, as was evidenced by the faint aroma of roasted pork and the aluminum foil-covered plate on the counter.

"What time is it?" I asked sleepily.

Laughing in step, my mother answered. "It's nearly ten o'clock at night. You have been out for a few hours. Julian carried you upstairs and tucked you in. I heard you had a big day."

Feeling famished, I tore the foil off and brought the lukewarm plate to the table. My mother scoffed and ripped it away to pop into the microwave.

"Yeah, I couldn't sleep. I went to the bakery early, and Julian needed my help setting up. I learned how to make doughnuts and turnovers, but I am not very good. I can do the custard though . . ." I trailed off on the exciting details of my morning.

Both of my parents smiled at my progress and willingness to go where the day took me. They inquired as to whether I intended on going back again. I hadn't thought about it, much less had a chance to ask Julian. I shrugged my shoulders and went about devouring my supper.

"If you want, you can come with me to meet Raina tomorrow. She's been waiting patiently to see you," my mother said enthusiastically.

Although I much prefer the busy activity of the bakery, the allure of meeting my mother's best friend was tempting. Knowing how ill she was, I knew it was in my best interest to take her up on the offer.

"I have heard so much about her, it would be nice to

actually meet her. Well, you know what I mean."

My mother smiled and clapped her hands lightly. "Oh, honey. This will make her day, I just know it."

After finishing my supper, I crawled back into bed and succumbed to the sleep my body craved. I did not overthink the upcoming day's events. After a day of hard work and mental stimulation, rest came easily. Several hours later, the sun was streaming into my bedroom brightly when my mother came to wake me. She spoke quietly, and brushed her fingers gently across my brow.

I smiled at her sweet face and sat up slowly. "Is it time for us to go?" I asked groggily.

"You have a little while, Stella. I made you breakfast, so you might want to shower and eat before we head out. I have quite a busy day, and do not typically get to stop before lunch."

I shifted slowly, turning my legs onto the edge of the bed and rubbed them to encourage circulation. They cramped slightly from the unusual activity, but loosened up after walking for a bit and running warm water over my body. On my way downstairs, I could smell the fried bacon and fluffy pancakes that were sitting on the table. My father had gone for the day, leaving me a banquet to sate my appetite. Like always, Julian was at the forefront of my mind. Knowing I would be meeting Raina compounded the questions I had swimming in my mind. What would she say to me? How did she feel about my return? My mother said she would be excited for my visit, but what kind of relationship did I have with her before I left town?

It was easier to just let the day unfold. Questions often answered themselves if I was quiet and listened. It was another beautiful day as we traveled to a secluded home on the water. It was tucked away down a long gravel road on a private cove of the lake, and tall trees shaded the property with privacy. What once appeared to be a trellis of grapes in the front, was now overgrown with weeds, and so was the rest of the yard. A hasty job of cutting the grass to keep it manageable was a testament to the strain on this home. A few cars were parked on the lawn next to the garage, one with a magnetic advertisement for a health care company on the side.

My mother began to explain who was already with Raina while we headed toward the back of the house. "She has twenty-four-hour care with nurse's aids. We know it's more comfortable here, and thankfully the bakery and vineyard bring in enough income to keep her home."

"Vineyard?" I immediately asked.

Nodding back toward the trellis, my mother's face tightened. "Yes, the family also operates a very successful winery a few miles from here. I am surprised Julian didn't say anything, since they sell the wine at the bakery."

Feeling confused, I wondered why it wasn't brought up before, and why Julian hadn't told me.

Sensing the thoughts in my mind, she continued to speak and answer my questions. "Perhaps he was busy, dear. Or maybe it's the fact that he is trying to find a buyer. Once Raina passes, Julian will return to New York. I know he's getting anxious, but he won't leave her before then. He doesn't have a family of his own, so there is nothing keeping him here, and it's a lot for one person to handle alone."

If the sudden heart break from being made aware of Julian's impending departure wasn't enough to wreck me, the moment I first laid eyes on Raina Moreau was enough to challenge all of the strength I thought I possessed. We entered through the back patio glass door and walked into the living room. A hospital bed was against the wall, facing out onto the lake for her to watch the day go by. I smiled to hide the fear gripping my soul. Her skin was pale and sunken around her dark-shadowed eyes. Thin, fragile arms rested across the blanket in her lap, with her tiny frame propped up on several pillows. The aide was sitting in a chair off to the side, gently massaging her limbs. I did not have to ask why. I knew cancer patients undergoing chemotherapy suffered from neuropathy, a condition where the limbs go numb. Aside from the comfort of physical touch, I imagined it helped with circulation.

My mother went over and kissed her gently on the cheek, as the women greeted each other joyfully. When she stopped to turn to me, I could see a light begin to radiate from Raina's eyes and the tears began to flow all around.

"Stella," she whispered.

I stood, unsure of what to do. I approached her slowly, then the aid offered her seat and introduced herself. "Hi, Stella. I'm Rebecca. I usually take care of Raina during the day. It's nice to meet you, but I am going to let you catch up."

She extended her hand. I shook it softly, then sat down. She asked if we would mind her setting up a few things for the next arrival. No one objected, and Raina's focus was brought back to me once again. She reached her delicate hand out in expectation. I accepted her request, and she brought it to her skeletal chest, pressing hard over her heart. I could feel the organ pulsing with life as she shook, softly weeping. I could not hold back my own tears from forming. I didn't know this woman, but my presence brought her something so deep even I knew this moment was one that transcended all understanding.

"Thank you, Jesus," she whispered.

Raising my brow curiously, I remained silent. Time seemed to slow down with the three of us together. Even my mother, with her full schedule, was solely focused on capturing the gift. I didn't want to move, yet my own arm was starting to fall asleep from the unnatural position. I gently slipped away, but held onto her grasp.

"Has Rebecca worked on your hands yet?" I asked Raina.

"No, not yet," she replied softly, while looking into the other room, in Rebecca's direction.

"Do you mind if I do it?"

Raina smiled and shook her head. "I'd like that very much."

Smiling brightly, I reached over and pumped a small amount of the lotion Rebecca was using into my palm. I took note it was fragrance free and hypoallergenic, and more memories surfaced on the care of cancer patients. No chemicals, sharp tools for the nails, or hair removal. Everything had to be the most gentle obtainable, because of how the chemotherapy wrecked the skin. A patient of my mother's once suffered a severe sunburn from less than twenty minutes in a car without protection. I massaged small circles over her fingers and up her arm toward her heart.

"She remembers some things, Sandy?" Raina questioned.

I shook my head and answered her myself. "No, I

don't. But I spent enough time at the hospital as a volunteer, and they would let me do things like this. I liked how relaxing it was to both me and the patients I visited. I had to complete a few trainings on technique and things to look for, so if I noticed something I could tell a nurse right away. Like this . . .''

Holding up her arm, I showed where a small bruise had formed from rubbing too hard.

"I'm sorry, Raina. I thought I was being gentle enough. Did that hurt? Do you want me to stop?"

Before I could pull my hand away, she reached over and grabbed it with the other. "Don't you dare, missy!"

My mother laughed loudly as I tentatively began to work on the other side.

Raina chuckled herself. "If you knew how much I missed you, you wouldn't have to question yourself. I know you don't remember me, but I've prayed long and hard for this day. I wouldn't have wished for the circumstances, but I won't complain. I never dreamed it would be at the same time as Julian. But God heard me, and here two you are."

I smiled and looked back at her. "Why is it so important that Julian be here, too?"

"Raina, don't!" My mother's panicked voice shrilled out and my head snapped.

The outburst did not move Raina. She reached to pull my hand into hers, and I was instantly able to see where Julian's intensity came from. Looking straight at me, she spoke to my mother. "Sandy, he is my son, and she needs to know this. It's going to come out, better she know now."

I felt the familiar anxiety creep up and the desire to flee grow feral, but I fought through the fear. Whatever it was, was important enough that Raina was willing to upset the balance. My mother took a deep breath, waiting for the words to cross her best friend's lips. I watched her chin quiver, and the grip on my palm tightened. I nodded for her to proceed, I couldn't deny this woman anything. More tears poured down both women's eyes as they looked at me with uncertainty. The wait was driving me mad, and I was ready to burst.

"Stella, there's something you need to know about Julian," Raina murmured.

Growing even more anxious, I wasn't sure how much longer I could sit still. Sensing my restlessness, she let out a deep breath and released my biggest fear.

Chapter 8

~ Unveiled ~

The truth about Julian and I was more than I was prepared to hear.

"You were the love of his life. And I have a feeling you still are. Being around you is very difficult for him. But for the first time in over a decade, I see a glimpse of my little boy. Who he was before going off to war. You may have just seen him for the first time yesterday, but he's been waiting a very long time to see you. Now I know that's probably a lot to take in, but I don't know how much longer I have, and I refuse to die leaving you in the dark."

Her words left me speechless, and brought my mother to her knees. The intensity of the situation had reached a climax, and I couldn't take another moment. I squeezed Raina's hands and apologized. "I . . . I am going to be outside. It was nice meeting you, Raina. I'm sorry, I just can't be here. I'm sorry."

I ignored the calls for me to stop, and sprinted down the hill toward the dock. Paying no attention to being fully clothed, I barreled full speed to the end of the wooden path and dove head first into the cool lake. The crashing of water, and then silence as my body floated to the top, bubbles tickling my face as they slipped from my lips, was enough to quiet the turmoil. When I broke the surface of the water, I screamed in agony. This wasn't happening, it couldn't be happening. I couldn't think of a more unimaginable cruelty. After hearing Raina speak, I knew she was right, no matter how much I hated it. There was only so long I could be around Julian before the past would refuse to stay hidden. What else would fight its way through, despite my desire to live in what Raina so perfectly addressed "the dark?"

Treading water, I slowly made my way back to the dock, then I hoisted myself onto the edge, catching my breath on the hard wooden planks. The sun quickly warmed my skin as I struggled to regain my composure. Covering my eyes with my arm, I listened to the steps on the dock as they approached. Anticipating it was my mother, or possibly Rebecca, checking on me, I remained in my spot. Not a word was said as the person sat quietly next to me, which meant only one thing. A moment later, I caught the distinct scent of the bakery in the breeze and turned my body away. The smell of comfort merely hours ago, was now one of torture.

"Why are you here?" I grumbled out.

He shifted in his seat, and I could hear the denim fibers rub against the wood grain, he was so close.

"Well, this is my house. But I was called," he replied flatly.

I pushed myself up, and sat looking across the lake, refusing to make eye contact with Julian.

"They shouldn't have bothered you. You have too much to worry about. You don't need to add me to it, especially since its hard being around me."

He pulled down the brim of his hat and washed his face with his hands, then growled loudly. "What did she tell you, Stella?"

I shook my head, furious. What good did it do me knowing the truth about a situation I couldn't change? I stood up and began to pace in small circles, waving my arms angrily. "That I'm your soul mate, or some shit. That you can't stand being around me, and it's driving her crazy. But don't worry, you don't have to play hero, Doc. I know soon enough I won't be your problem. You can forget all about me and this town, and go back to your important life where you can save the day."

By time I finished, Julian was in my face, staring down hard at me, but not saying a word. For every step I took back, he moved forward.

"Stella, stop." He hissed.

"You don't know anything. You don't even know me, so just stop."

My arms instinctively reacted, and pushed him off the side of the dock into the water. As he surfaced, I remained infuriated and shouted back. "If I knew how to stop it, don't you think I would? I didn't ask her to tell me that. She insisted, even when my mom told her not to. But you know what, it doesn't matter, because it's not me. I might have her body, but I don't have her memories. You are right, I don't know you, and whatever you had with her is gone, and I certainly know enough not to believe you would ever feel that way about me now."

I stormed off toward the house, and refused to turn

around, even though I could hear the water splash as he climbed up the ladder. My mother and Rebecca were standing on the porch observing the heated exchange. I was soaking wet, but walked directly to the car and leaned against the side with folded arms. Julian moved onto the porch, past the women, and into the house. My mother followed him inside, and more confrontation took place among the group. I felt incredibly guilty that Julian could be so upset with Raina. I could only imagine where she was in her plight. I wanted to be angry at her, but I wasn't. She loved her son, and she was protecting him.

Julian emerged with dry clothes, and said nothing has he hopped back in his truck. He drove away in haste, spinning rocks in every direction as the wheels caught traction. My mother came out a bit later, with red, swollen eyes, and also remained silent as she stepped into her SUV. She took me back to our house without asking if I wanted to finish the rounds with her. I wanted to console her, but I had probably embarrassed her with my behavior. I knew the only way to make this right was to settle things with Julian. But first, I needed to make amends with Raina. I changed my clothes when my mother left, then began the walk a few miles down the road back to the Moreau's home. I wasn't sure what would come next, but it had to be better than this.

Chapter 9

~ Dry Land ~

The long walk gave me time to collect my thoughts and reflect on my behavior. Hopefully Raina was an understanding woman. Then again, she had to be, why else would she force the issue? It took about an hour to reach the edge of the gravel road that led down to the house. From a different view, I could see the hidden beauty of the property. Birds called out from all around as I meandered under the trees, through beams of sunshine illuminating the forest floor. It was the first walk during the day that I had taken alone, and I vowed to continue exploring the sprawling village along the lake.

Rebecca's car was no longer parked, and had been replaced by another bearing the same health care emblem. I walked around to the back door, lightly tapped on the glass, and waited for someone to answer. Raina saw me, and immediately called for her next aid to let me in. Giving a knowing smile, she beckoned me forward to take a seat.

Before approaching the bedside, I began my apology.

"Raina, I am so sorry. I shouldn't have done that. I . . . I just didn't know what to do." I breathed out heavily and plopped onto the chair next to her.

Curiously she looked out at the patio. "Where is Sandy?" she asked.

I shrugged my shoulders. "On her rounds. I went home and changed, then came right back here. I couldn't stand to see her so upset, and I knew I needed to talk to you."

Raina reached out her hand for me, which I accepted without question. Squeezing affectionately, she laughed. "Stella, if you were not upset, I would be more concerned. I prefer to face challenges head on, rather than let them simmer into a bigger issue. This town knew who you and Julian were as a couple. I would hate for you to find out any other way. Although I love the idea of seeing you together, I have no delusions about the situation. He still carries a tremendous amount of love for you around with him, as do I, and your mama told me that there is no telling if and when your memory will come back."

I nodded my head in agreement at the statement.

"Do you want to know more, Stella?" she asked quietly.

Of course I did. Now that the door had been opened, my curiosity was no longer manageable. It was unfair of me to ask everyone not to tell me who I was because of actions I couldn't remember. I only had one request. "Raina, I do, but I am not sure how much I am ready for yet."

She smiled brightly and pointed to the shelf against the wall lined with thick photo albums. "Of course, I will only go as far as you want, Stella. Please bring me the dark red one. It's a favorite of mine."

I grazed my fingers along the plastic covered spines, feeling the aged cracks as I trailed to the one she desired. Before opening the book, I could see how the pages had yellowed over time, despite the sleeves protecting the paper memories. I sat down and propped the heavy book on my knees, to where Raina could see them, and opened the cover. The first two pictures I saw caused the breath to catch in my throat and my eyes to well up. It was one of me, just shortly after leaving Ohio, standing next to a younger Julian in formal wear. His hair was longer than it is now, with a slight curl. My dress was light pink with layers of tulle, and rhinestones across the strapless bodice. Julian was wearing a black suit, with a matching pink tie and kerchief sticking out of his pocket.

We both laughed while turning each page and exploring the past. Julian and I were so carefree, often making silly faces in the photos. I didn't remember any of it, but that didn't mean it wasn't good. Like my mother had told me, I was happy, and it was because of him.

"How did we meet, Raina? Julian and I?" I asked with a grin.

Raina laughed loudly and flipped a few pages to the image of Julian and me on a boat. Our hair was drenched, clinging to our faces, and dripping down onto the bright orange life jackets with the sun setting behind us. The smiles on our face were bright.

"Julian heard that a pretty new girl had moved to town and liked to sunbathe topless on her deck because she thought no one could see her. But if you had a boat, you could quietly putter into the cove, and if you were lucky, you would catch a glimpse of her."

My eyes grew wide as my mouth gaped open. I could see myself doing something like that to avoid tan lines. Knowing it was a town rumor brought a flush to my cheeks.

"So that doesn't explain how we met." I giggled.

Raising her brows, she continued to flip to the next page where there was a barbeque and my parents were grilling out. Julian was sitting next to his mother, eating at the picnic table.

"He wasn't content just seeing you from a distance, so he tied to your parents dock and went up to the porch to introduce himself. You screamed and ran inside embarrassed, but he waited on the dock for you to come back out. For three days straight. Both of your parents thought he had lost his mind, and your father threatened to call the police. However, Sandy thought it was a very romantic gesture, and eventually convinced you to talk to him. When you finally did, he was never the same again, and you two were inseparable."

I touched the image affectionately, while more questions began to surface. "But we did separate. My mom told me that I went away to school and he joined the Navy. Why didn't he stay here to help you take care of things?"

Raina's hand grazed mine lightly. "Because of you. It takes a strong man to support a woman with big dreams. He knew he would need more than money to love you. His heart is like yours, and you were devoted to making the world a better place. He knew you would be gone for a long while, and it seemed the best solution for him to bide his time. When my husband Romain was alive, we were fine. It was only after he passed that I became ill and Julian felt obligated to return."

A heaviness fell over us as we flipped more pages. Julian's boot camp pictures, my first lab coat with the UNC logo, his deployment party. Suddenly, the pictures of me were gone. It was only Julian, and he looked much different. His face was weathered, sunken, and cold.

"He looks so much older in these ones," I said with a deep sadness.

Raina nodded her head and closed the book. "War changes people. He almost died. Julian was traveling with a group of Marines to another post when a roadside IED went off and killed two other men in the unit. Julian was knocked unconscious, and a fellow soldier pulled him to safety. He spent quite some time in the hospital getting better. They gave him a leave of absence for the holidays, and he was able to come home."

Setting the book off to the edge, she tilted her head and called for Weston, her next aid, to administer her medication. "I am so sorry Stella, but we must stop there. I am very tired. Perhaps you will come back again in few days. I've missed you."

Weston had already prepared the medication and administered it into her port. Within moments, she was sound asleep. Several hours had passed, and the sun was starting to set. I picked up the photo album, and a folded newspaper clipping slipped out of the back and fell to my feet. I bent over slightly to pick it up, and curiosity got the best of me. As my eyes scanned the large bold print, the album went crashing to the ground with a loud thud. The noise did not wake Raina, and Weston stepped back into the room to see what had happened.

Smiling lightly, I picked up the book and walked it to the shelf. "I accidently dropped this." I laughed.

He nodded and went back to working at his laptop in the kitchen. I folded the article into a palm sized square and slipped it into my pocket for further inspection at a later time. I said goodbye to Weston, then excused myself and started the walk back home. Before I reached the end of the driveway, Julian pulled in quickly, slamming on his brakes once the headlights hit my body, and fish tailing in the gravel. I froze in the middle of the road only a few feet away from the large grill of the truck.

Without turning off the engine, Julian opened the door and stomped toward me. "What the hell are you doing here? I almost hit you!"

Annoyed and frightened by his aggressive behavior, I jumped back into his face. "You should be paying attention! What if I were a deer or something?"

"You aren't a fucking deer, though!" He growled.

Julian paced back and forth under the bright lights that were casting long shadows against the trees. Upset by the possibility something terrible could have occurred, he breathed in and out forcefully to calm down. I didn't want to fight with him anymore.

Hoping to stop his frantic thoughts, I moved to keep him from walking any further and grabbed his face on both sides. "Julian, I am okay. Look at me," I said sternly.

His eyes were wild and lost. I wasn't sure what else to do, so I wrapped my arms around him and pulled him close. His body shook in my embrace, and his arms pulled me even tighter.

I repeated myself, but this time in a whisper, "Julian, I am okay."

He wasn't ready to let me go for a long while, and I did

not try to break away. I waited for his breathing to slow, and ran my fingers along his neck in slow, soothing motions.

He stepped back and brought my chin up to meet his gaze. "Stella, I'm sorry. I just can't believe I almost ran you over. I didn't know you were here." His voice cracked out.

I tried to smile and hugged him again briefly. "Does this make us even?" I laughed.

I felt a shiver as his hands trailed slowly down my spine, then his nose buried into the crook of my neck and nuzzled gently.

"No, this doesn't make us even. Shoving me off the dock just hurt my pride. I deserved it. It's going to take me a little while to come down after this." Julian's hands were shaking with adrenaline. The sharp muscles in his jaw flexed as he clenched it tightly, and his pupils were encompassing the entire iris—he was in a nearly feral state.

"What can I do to calm you down?" I asked.

His labored breathing was not letting up. He walked to his truck, turned off the engine, and shut the doors. He grabbed my hand gently, and we walked down the path to the dock in the scant moonlight. Julian knew the trail by memory, and avoided the rocks and large roots that were potentially hazardous. I remained quiet as he guided me onto the sleek cigarette speedboat, then stepped in himself before untying the ropes and lifting the side bumpers. The twin engines fired with a purr, and we glided onto the black glass lake away from the world. Once past the no-wake zone, Julian told me to sit down or hold on. Unsure of what to grasp onto, I settled into the plush seat next to him. He pushed the throttle forward. The boat lifted, and began to fly into the night. A bright GPS system guided him where his eyes could not see, as lights on the boat warned others of our approach.

I watched Julian's face remain like stone, lit up by the blue-hued screen. Occasionally he would glance toward me, holding my stare before looking back out into the darkness. Along the banks of the water, large luxurious homes dotted the landscape. For whatever reason, we appeared to be the only ones out in the early evening, which seemed strange for the late spring. It was only a Wednesday, however, and I had seen how busy it became on the weekends. We turned into a large, dark cove. Julian dropped anchor and turned off the engine.

"I'll be right back, okay?" he said before disappearing below the deck.

He returned with a bundle of blankets and pillows, and set them on a seat while making the back bench row pull out into a flat bed. I watched tentatively as he stretched the blankets out, unsure of what he was doing.

Sensing my uncertainty, he spoke without looking up. "Don't worry, Stella. I will get you back tonight. I just thought you might like to see this." He patted the bed and encouraged me to lay down next to him. The moment my head hit the pillow, I gasped. Above us, the night sky was so bright and brilliant, unlike anything I had ever seen before. There were so many stars, I was unable to comprehend how small I felt.

"Oh my god, Julian. This is amazing! Is this what calms you down? You need to bring me out here more often! Look, there's the Big Dipper, and Taurus!"

I turned my head, and Julian was not looking into the

night sky, but directly at me.

"What? Why are you looking at me?" I asked with a smile.

He slowly lifted his hand to graze my cheek, and my eyes fluttered closed under his touch. Light fingers swept along the edge of my ear, down my neck, across my jaw, and over my lips. "I am thinking about what you said on the dock earlier. How you think I would never look at you that way."

Swallowing hard, I opened my eyes. "I shouldn't have said that. It was just presumed. I know we were really happy together. I feel better knowing that I met you and we were in love. I don't like not knowing what happened to tear us apart, but I also know that I am not that same person."

Julian's brow furrowed. He moved his body to fully turn on his side, and I could smell the sweet yeast and sugar from the bakery. It was like an aphrodisiac, covering my brain in a blanket of warmth. He noticed me edge a bit closer and inhaled once again deeply, laughing slightly.

"How do you know we were happy, Stella?" he asked curiously.

I was unsure if he could see how much my face lit up.

"I came back and apologized to your mom for freaking out. She asked if I wanted to know about us. We looked at pictures and she let me ask questions. For as much as I don't want to know what happened, it is actually making me feel better to know what kind of life I had here. Before we moved I was so scared, and it feels like it was yesterday my mom told me we were coming down here. My whole life was ripped away. It means a lot knowing I was okay, that I found you."

Julian's breathing increased, but not out of fear for my safety. I rubbed his arm affectionately and curled into his chest. Rather than yielding to my touch, his body grew frigid and rolled away.

"I better get you back before your parents worry too much. I can bring you here again sometime if you like. It's best when the moon is low, but even when it's full it's pretty nice."

Julian held out his hand and helped me down, then quickly pulled the blankets off of the berth and tossed them down the hole. Something had changed in him, but I dared not ask what. His battles were just as fierce as mine, just in a completely different way. If he wanted to open up to me, it would have to be his choice. Just as he wouldn't force me, I had to offer the same respect. He fired up the boat once more, and flew in a new direction, across the lake to my parents' dock. Seeing the house from a new perspective made me try to imagine Julian approaching for the first time, in hopes of catching a glimpse of me. Wondering if the same thoughts crossed his mind, a sadness washed over me. For every step I took forward, I took two more back. I thought he was just going to drop me off, and was surprised when he tied to the edge.

"You don't have to come up, Julian. I will be okay. The path is paved."

He raised his eyebrows and chuckled deeply. "Yeah, I just drop you off and Mr. Brady will have my ass. Trust me, you do not want to be on the receiving end of his wrath."

I wanted to laugh, but my jaw simply clenched, remembering dinner a few nights before and what I had told him. I knew all too well the coldness my father could possess.

Realizing the mistake in his words, although innocent, he pulled me into a hug. "Stella, I'm sorry. You do know, so you understand. I won't give him an excuse to keep us from seeing each other."

I laughed into his chest. "God, you would swear I really was seventeen, not in my thirties. I need to do something so I stop getting treated like a child."

Julian reached for my hand and walked slowly up the concrete stairs. "You are most definitely not a child. I know they feel responsible for you, as do I. It will get better. You are just starting to leave the house. The more you exert your independence, the more they will trust you are okay."

I squeezed his hand and stopped him before reaching the top step. "Can I see you tomorrow?" I questioned hopefully.

Being so close to the house, I could see his face fully under the lamp. Slowly, his lip curved into a sly grin. "You can see me whenever you want. Just not in front of my truck scaring the shit of me. Can you manage that?"

I balled my fists by my sides and stomped my foot. "Are you kidding me? Watch how fast you are going!"

Julian raised his hands in defeat and backed away. "Fair enough." He laughed.

My parents must have heard us exchanging words, because Sandy walked out of the back door with a smile on her face.

"Hey mom, sorry I didn't call to tell you where I was. I hope I didn't scare you."

She shook her head and smiled. "Weston sent me a

text while you and Raina were talking. I assumed you were with Julian. Both of you need to come in here."

We looked at each other, and I started to grow tense. Julian rubbed my back to assure me it was going to be okay. As I followed both of them into the house, we walked into the kitchen where my mother had us sit at the table.

"Mom, what's going on?" I asked tentatively.

She turned around and smiled, then pulled down two plates, setting them down in front of us.

"Oh, nothing. I was just messing with you. Are you hungry?"

Chapter 10

~ Prey ~

After dinner, I walked Julian down to the dock to say goodbye. Although it wasn't necessary, I found it harder and harder to let him walk away from me. Less than a week had passed since our paths crossed that morning, and I had already formed an attachment to him. Holding the flashlight cord and swinging it back and forth as he pulled the buoys in, I felt like a lost puppy. I shook my head and turned around, then started the walk back to the house.

"Hey, Stella. Wait!"

I looked over my shoulder, but wouldn't turn around. This was ridiculous, he wasn't leaving forever. "Yeah?" I replied casually.

The look on his face told me he wasn't buying it. He tilted his head curiously, and I watched as his eyes scanned me from head to toe.

"Goodnight, Stella," he said softly.

I nodded my head and started walking again. The engine did not turn until I closed the glass door and turned off the light. Still sitting at the kitchen table with a mug of tea, my mother peered over her glasses and patted the seat next to her. She breathed out deeply, then took my hand and squeezed.

Despite taking a sip of tea before speaking, her voice remained cracked. "I need to apologize to you, Stella. I've been reluctant to tell you anything, for fear it would do more harm than good. I know I was upset with Raina, but I am glad she did it, and I am glad you went back. She has more courage than I do. I just would never want to see your heart broken again."

I reached over and hugged my mom, consoling her with the fact that we were in this together. With damp faces, we laughed and created a mound of tissues on the table.

I felt a little more bravery surface before sleep would come calling, and took the chance while it was there. "Mama, were Julian and I intimate?" I asked embarrassed.

She nearly spit her tea across the table, not expecting that particular question. "Um. Why do you ask?" she choked out.

Watching my mother squirm under the inquiry made me feel devious. It wasn't my intention, but it spoke volumes without saying a word.

"Just curious." I laughed.

She shook her head, took another drink and prepared to reply, then hesitated. "Stella, there are some things that neither Raina nor I should tell you when it comes to Julian. Now that you are aware of your past, I believe those types of things should come from him, not us."

I was frustrated at being denied more information, I had become greedy with knowledge. Most of all, I wanted to know why Julian reacted the way he did with me. Could he really look at me the same way he did when we were younger? For as much as I wanted to hope, the dark voice in the back of my head reminded me not to get too comfortable. This could all be over in a blink. Lying down, I cried myself to sleep, rather than indulge in thoughts of a future that didn't belong to me.

After some restless sleep, I once again awoke before dawn and started the trek to the bakery to keep myself occupied. While picking the dead leaves out of the hanging flower pots, I heard Julian cough as he approached. Every step he took matched the thump in my chest, with each beat harder the closer he came.

"Good morning," he said in a sultry drawl.

My heartbeat skipped and I turned away embarrassed.

Concern hit Julian and he palmed my shoulders. "Stella, what's wrong?"

I shook my head and refused to make eye contact. "It's stupid," I hissed through clenched teeth.

He used his hand to gently lift my chin, and I knew he wouldn't let this go.

"Nothing is stupid, talk to me."

Rather than fighting my feelings, I put them out there, and prepared to get shot down. They weren't going away, and only amplified with each passing hour. "I have a problem. I really like you. I know it's foolish, but I can't shut it off. I shouldn't have come here today. I'm sorry, you don't need this right now."

Tears welled in my eyes, but Julian grabbed my arm as

I started to bolt. His voice came out somewhat cold and distant. He was in doctor mode. "Stella, you can't help how you feel, but that doesn't make it foolish. I am glad you told me, and I hope you don't regret it. I know it must have changed things to know who we used to be together, but I can't be that person to you right now. It doesn't mean I still don't want to be your friend, so please don't leave or shut me out. I can help you work through those feelings if you want me to."

I nodded and wiped my face. He was absolutely right, even though that wasn't the answer I wanted. "Yeah, sure," I replied quietly.

While pulling pans out and measuring flour and sugar for the donuts, Julian started to ask me questions. "Tell me how you feel physically when you see me."

I started to blush, unsure how to answer, and even more embarrassed to confess it. I know he meant well, and I definitely needed to get over this, so I let it out. "I can't breathe. My heart rate speeds up, my stomach goes into knots. I feel clammy."

Julian's face was flat and without emotion while listening to my symptoms. If he felt anything toward me like I had previously thought, he wasn't giving anything away in this moment. More emotions surfaced, and despite him not addressing the first set, I continued to tell him how I felt. "Right now, I feel sick and inadequate. I am ashamed, and I want nothing more than to run. But I know I can't keep running away."

I punched the dough down hard and my fist hit the steel prep table. I cried out, and immediately Julian came over to check on me. Anger still lurched in my veins and I spit out venomously as he approached. "Stay away from me. I'm fine."

I held my sore arm close, then walked to the ice chest with a dish cloth and made a poultice to ease the swelling. Terry must have been waiting outside, as the swinging doors cracked timidly. Julian waved him in with a deep exhalation. Silently, he went about his duties in the middle of the standoff. I walked out and sat on the steps, watching the sunrise with tears streaming down my face. I was a complete wreck, and none of this was helping me feel better.

Shortly thereafter, Julian sat next to me and spoke in the same clinical tone. "Stella, just like you had to relearn how to do some things physically, you have to work on them emotionally. For the past few months, you have been sheltered for the most part, and only given a little bit of the truth at time. Even in the past, you hid your emotions out of fear. You have the choice, as you said, to keep running from them, or facing them head on. You need to learn how to channel them, and know which feelings are appropriate, and which are not. Your impulsive nature can be tamed and used for good, or it can destroy you."

I continued to look off into the distance, only moving my head as Julian pulled my hand into his lap to inspect the bruising on my knuckles.

"I am not rejecting you, Stella. I know it feels that way, but it's not true. I just refuse to hurt you. I hope you can understand that."

I nodded silently and looked at my swollen hand. The skin had split in a few places, and was searing with pain. I didn't realize I'd hit it that hard.

"The amygdala is a bitch, Stella." Julian chuckled.

I looked at him curiously, then rewrapped my hand and

stood to walk inside. "What do you mean?"

"It's the part of your brain that rules your emotions. It's not the sympathetic nervous system that makes you feel the sweaty palms and rapid heartbeat. The amygdala is a huge component when dealing with emotion, especially fear and memory."

I walked to the sink and allowed the cool water to run over my hand, then turned to Julian. "So you believe the way I feel about you is simply brain chemistry? It's not real?"

His face dropped then quickly went blank. "Stella, everything is real, but that doesn't mean it's what's best. Your brain is responding the stimuli it's encountering. From an evolutionary standpoint, I represent safety, sexual attraction, which leads to reproduction, stability, and protection. All things necessary for the survival of offspring. Being older, your biology is different than when you were seventeen. You are contending with mature hormones, and carefully honed genetics."

I turned the faucet off and lightly dried my hand, then walked past him to the ice machine once more. "A simple yes would have done just fine, doctor."

I could tell he wanted to continue the conversation, but more work was needed to get the bakery up and running. Unlike the previous morning I was there, Terry was not in a joking mood and worked quickly to make up for the time lost with our spat. I walked out of the kitchen and into the main area to clean fingerprints off the glass displays, restock napkins, and start the morning coffee. Julian let me be, and within an hour, the bakery was buzzing with the morning's regulars.

My hand started to throb, but I refused to let it get to

me. I carefully put the soiled mugs and plates from the patio tables into the plastic bussing carts. While I was cleaning off one table, a gentleman at the one next to it removed his sunglasses and sat up.

"Stella Brady, is that you?" he asked.

Thinking it was someone from the town I hadn't seen in a while, I smiled brightly. "Yep, sure is." I laughed.

The man stood to shake my hand, but I reached out the hand opposite the one he was extending. He looked down and saw the bruising on my knuckles and gave a look of concern.

"Get in a brawl there, little lady? Good to know you still got it." He chuckled.

I furrowed my brow and sighed. "Yes, the rye bread dough took one of my right hooks like a champ."

He chuckled again, but uncomfortably. I noticed he kept looking behind me, but each time I went to look, he quickly started speaking, gathering my attention again. "So Stella, you're working at this bakery now? That's quite a change."

I shook my head. "I am just keeping myself busy. I don't get paid or anything. I just enjoy meeting everyone."

Right then, I heard two men get into a shouting match. I turned to see Julian holding a large camera. He pulled something out of it and put it into his pocket, before smashing the camera on the ground. The man talking to me ran over and joined in the argument, as Julian stormed toward me, pulling me into the bakery and locking the door.

Angrily, he shouted for me not to leave, and instructed the staff to shut everything down before charging back outside. I listened to the altercation taking place between the three men before hearing sirens coming in the distance. The words "reporter," "privacy," and "lawsuit" were shouted before the police finally forced the men to step away. Julian remained outside with the police for several more moments, before coming in shaking with fury, walking straight into the kitchen, and throwing things around angrily. The officer stood inside the front door and observed for a few minutes, before asking if I was Stella Brady. Julian came back out and appeared a bit calmer, but his nostrils were still flared defensively.

"Julian, I need to talk to Miss Brady alone, mind if I use the kitchen?" The officer asked.

He didn't verbally respond, just simply held his hand toward the door before going behind the counter to help the others finish closing early. I followed the officer into the kitchen, apprehensive of what was about to be asked.

"Miss Brady, I am Sheriff Newman. I need to ask you a few questions about the man who was talking to you a bit ago. Do you know who he was?"

I shook my head. "No, I just assumed he was someone from the town that I didn't remember. Why?" Sheriff Newman scrawled a few things down on a small notebook before continuing. "What was he talking to you about?"

I shrugged and tried to recall the conversation. "Not much, just asked about me working at the bakery, and my hand. I explained that I'd punched the bread dough too hard and it hit the table. But he did make a comment that it was good I still had it. I didn't think much of it."

A few more things were written down before another question came. "Did you notice the man doing anything odd while you were talking to him?"

I remembered the man's behavior and nodded. "Yes. He was looking off in the direction of where Julian and that man got into the fight. I wasn't sure what he was looking at, and every time I turned around, he would say something that would make me start talking again."

"So you didn't actually see the man until after the fight started?"

"No, I didn't. I heard the shouting, and the man went over while Julian pulled me into the bakery. What happened?"

Sheriff Newman closed his notebook and slipped it into his front pocket. Then he took off his light grey hat, and rubbed his balding head before putting it back down. "Well, ma'am. It appears he was a celebrity reporter of some sort, doing a scoop on you. Julian must have seen the photographer hiding and grabbed his camera before the guy took off. Now I don't condone damage to someone's property, but considering how you got hurt, I am taking Julian's side on this."

My eyes widened at the sheriffs comment. "You know how I got hurt?"

His face was sad as he placed his right hand on my shoulder gently. "Stella, there isn't much about your life that isn't on the internet. Nobody knew you were down here until recently, so you haven't been exposed to these vultures. We will do the best we can to protect you, but you really need to start watching out for yourself. You can't be going out alone anymore, and your parents should probably get a security system on their place. I know it's an inconvenience, but we hear stories about this stuff all the time. People are crazy."

I wanted to cry, but remembered what Julian told me.

I needed to channel my feelings. "What else can I do? I don't want to be a burden here."

The sheriff called Julian into the kitchen. I could see his nerves were shot, and felt the tension when he came over to me immediately and opened his arms for a hug. After releasing me, his hands scoured my face for a phantom injury.

"I'm okay, Julian. Are you, is the question."

He closed his eyes and brought his lips to my forehead, pressing softly. I felt warmth radiate through my veins. This feeling, I would not try to control.

"Yeah, I will be alright."

Sheriff Newman stood by quietly, and waited for us to turn to him before speaking. "Julian, we need to call a town meeting. Someone notified that buzzard to Stella's whereabouts. It doesn't appear she gave him any indication about her amnesia, but if it does come out, we need to set up a plan of protection. I have a feeling that was only the tip of the iceberg, and our little town is about to start swarming with those assholes."

Julian groaned loudly. "Let's do it tonight."

Chapter 11

~ Fight or Flight ~

The ride to my parents' house was quiet, as Julian drove quickly. They greeted us at the door and ushered us in. Sheriff Newman called them, and started to discuss the topics for the town meeting that would take place that evening. I listened to it all in a haze, disbelieving something like this was happening. Just when I started to venture out into the world, I was being shuttered back behind closed doors. Was this the life I really had before? Never getting to live like other people, no freedom to walk without someone hiding in the bushes taking pictures. Or even getting to talk to a stranger out of kindness, without worry of ulterior motives? How sad my existence must have been. I looked down at a tattoo on my inner arm that I always questioned. It was a birdcage with a padlock. It now made sense.

Julian sat protectively next to me, either with his arm around my back, or his hand resting on my thigh. I would exchange glances with my mother at the possessive behavior. We both hid our smiles behind the seriousness of the situation. Between Julian, my father, and the town sheriff, they would do everything in their power to keep me safe.

"Stella, you can't walk to the bakery alone anymore, or anywhere else for that matter."

My father's words sunk deep, despite already knowing them to be true. "I know, daddy."

For the first time since I came back, his instinct to protect me overrode any apprehension he held. At the end of the day, I was still his child. The love and concern being poured over me made me realize how much they all truly cared, despite the past. Without thinking about it, I leaned my head onto Julian's shoulder, then he turned and gently kissed the top of my head affectionately.

"You'll be okay, I promise," he said.

I smiled at the comforting words, then gathered my things to head off and see the sheriff before the meeting. The mayor and small police force were all present to discuss the plan of action. Rather than sitting at the large wooden table, I sat off to the side with my mother, as Julian, with his military training, stepped forward and told them how things would take place. His experience in war and strategy was not questioned, and everyone agreed to the protocols he wanted in place.

"We don't have the funds for private security, Julian. We are not going to spend taxpayer's hard-earned money to protect her. I know she's famous, but we have to think about our town," one man shouted.

Unmoved, Julian tilted his head and calmly explained. "Miss Brady's financial advisor has already contacted Stella's former guardians, and they will be arriving very shortly. No special protection will be necessary from the town's end. Please understand these are highly trained men who have been with Miss Brady for a very long time, and they know exactly how to work in situations like this. We are simply letting you know what is going to take place so we are all on the same page. Is that understood?"

This part of the plan I found particularly interesting. I had yet to encounter anyone from my old life. Knowing that they had been with me closely would give me the opportunity to find out more about what kind of person I was, and perhaps solve the mystery of why I disappeared. Within the hour, eight men dressed in immaculately tailored suits arrived in the conference room. One of the men was particularly large. I imagine he was over six-foot-seven, and nearly three hundred pounds of muscle. He looked like a linebacker, but his eyes conveyed something much softer. As the meeting started, I stood up and walked over to the intimidating man. The room grew silent as he stood, towering over me by a solid foot.

"What is your name sir?" I asked.

"Christopher Matthew, ma'am," he replied sharply.

I took another step closer and watched his chest rise as he held in his breath. "How long have you worked with me?"

He looked down, and I could see the restraint in his face. "Six years, ma'am."

I smiled and looked around the room, before leaning in and whispering, "You want to give me a hug, don't you?"

I smiled mischievously at Christopher, and watched him let out the breath. I imagined such a request from his end would be breaking a serious protocol, something inside told me he needed it.

"Yes, ma'am," he choked out.

I reached out my arms and took one last step forward. My arms barely reached around his back, while his were all encompassing and swallowed me whole. I did not know this man, but my heart instantly gravitated toward him. I looked at the others, and they all held the same look of longing. I felt my body wracking with sobs at each embrace. Finally sitting down again, I wiped my eyes as the entire room zeroed in on me.

"I don't remember you guys, and I am so sorry for that. But for some, reason I know you care about me. I feel like you're my family, and I am home. I know that sounds crazy, but it's true."

I hid my head in my hands and cried.

Julian came over and pulled me into his arms. "You aren't crazy, Stella. It's why I asked these men to come. They know you like the back of their hands. They didn't hesitate to come here, because they care about you the same way we do."

I looked at the men gratefully, and apologized for interrupting the meeting. Something in that moment broke, and they actually started to smile, including the mayor and other police officers. Perhaps it was seeing I wasn't the spoiled brat they probably imagined. I was a real person who needed their help.

Several hours went by, and the entire town hall filled with residents concerned about how my arrival would impact things. No one had bothered me up until this point. They'd all been respectful of my mother and the abundance of race car drivers who liked their privacy. Knowing so little about the person I was now became a disadvantage. I had to face up to who I became if there was any hope of me surviving. After the meeting was adjourned and the plans voted upon, they immediately went into effect. The security team assigned shifts and would start the securing of my parents property tonight. Before leaving for the evening, I asked to meet privately with the guards. Julian nodded to my parents that it would be okay. If they were protecting me, I needed to trust them, even though I already did with every fiber of my being. Once more, the men took seats around the table in the conference room. Rather than taking a seat myself, I crawled up on the table and sat cross legged in the center.

It took a moment to think about what exactly I wanted to say. Formulating words with eloquence was not something that came easily to me. The past few days had thrown me into a whirlwind, and I needed to know I was anchored to something unmovable. Julian had far too much on his plate to stay so concerned, which was another reason I imagine he called in the team.

Anxiously, I began picking at my nails before looking at the group of men. "I don't really know what to say, except I am sure you know by now that I have amnesia. There isn't anything I can recall before the age of seventeen, but I have these moments where I think I remember something, like tonight. I get really frustrated because I struggle so much, but I am getting better every day. I don't really know much about who I was when you were with me, and neither do they, outside of magazines and the internet. I refuse to look because I don't know what is true."

Warm tears streaked my face, but the group did not look bothered. "I don't think I was very happy. I mean, I know I wasn't happy. I have a feeling I did some really awful things, and if that includes things I may have done to you, I am sorry. If I can make it up, please let me try and fix it, because I need your help to know the truth."

Deep, ragged breaths forced from my lungs while I fought to gain my composure. Another gentleman handed me a tissue and, one by one, they introduced themselves and told me a bit about who they were. First there was Michael, who was a former Marine, and had taken me on as a client and was my lead guardian for seven years. From there it was Christopher, Todd, Robert, Jason, Bryan, Truman, and Noah. All varying times of service, but none less than four years. I was moved by their devotion to my wellbeing and the willingness to come at such short notice.

Truman chuckled under his breath. "It kind of sucks working for other people. With you, we knew what we were going to get, and you took great care of us. Honestly, you weren't much trouble, compared to some other clients. I think we all knew it was a front. Being here, we get to understand more about you, too. You have always been a good person, Stella. Sometimes you could be a real bitch to others, but never to us. Besides Vida, I think we were the only people you trusted."

I let out a sigh of relief and then asked, "Who is Vida?"

Michael looked at Truman and shook his head, before answering me himself, "She was your manager, Stella, but I highly suggest leaving her be. After your accident, she became a loose cannon. We never really trusted her, but it wasn't our place to speak out."

Crossing my arms, and then looking down while nodding my head, I replied.

"Well, I trust you, and so does Julian. If you say to leave it be, consider it done. However, I need to know what she looks like. If she shows up here, I want to be able to alert someone. I have a feeling I will be pretty hidden from now on, but this morning shows me that I can't be too careful."

I shifted my body to scoot off the table, and Christopher stood to help me down. "Well, aren't you chivalrous? I think I will keep you around."

I grinned brightly, and walked to the exit with the men following behind me. I saw Julian's eyes pass over me, and scan the men with discernment. Instantly, we saw something about one another that had yet to surface— who we both were before returning to Mooresville, after we had parted. The people we had become was bound to collide with the ones that were currently in states of limbo. We walked outside, and a large black SUV was waiting. Christopher held the door for me. Confused, I looked to Julian for direction.

"This is how it has to be, Stella. They are your guardians now. Don't worry, I am right behind you."

Slowly, I stepped into the truck, and each man took a seat. I stared at the floor the entire short distance to my parents' house, listening to them catch up. Upon arriving, a security company was already busy installing cameras, sensors, and alarms throughout the house and property. Our dining room had become a command center, with multiple computers and monitors. Feeling panic overcome me, I ran to the bathroom and slammed the door, then sunk to the ground.

A soft knock came to the door and I could hear his voice. "Stella, will you please let me in? Let me talk to you," Julian said calmly.

I cracked the door, but remained sitting against the

cool porcelain tub. Moving next to me but not touching me, Julian used his most soothing voice to explain what was happening. "It's only for tonight, Stella. I know it's overwhelming. They needed a place to start monitoring, but they will relocate in the morning. I don't think you quite understand who you are. Unfortunately, this is necessary to protect you."

Numbly, I asked Julian for respite. "Take me to the cove, please. I don't want to be here tonight."

He paused in consideration, and then leaned in to brush the hair away from my eyes. "I think that's a good idea, too. Pack some clothes. I will go get the boat and be right back. Give me an hour."

I nodded in agreement and quickly thought of Raina. "Julian, your house needs monitoring, too. Send someone over to keep watch. Everything they are doing here, they need to do there. I insist."

He closed his eyes, taking in the ramifications of being a part of my world. With all of this concern on my behalf, we could not discount the vulnerability of his properties. If I had to seclude myself away to a life of isolation, I preferred to know I could still visit her in safety.

"Okay, Stella. I'll send them over as soon as they finish here. I will be right back, I promise."

I smiled and took his hand to stand, then reached around his waist and pulled him close.

"Thank you, Julian. I would be lost without you."

He laughed and hugged back. "I think that goes both ways."

Julian quickly left the house after instructing the security installment company to cover his property when they finished. Being able to give his mother fair warning of what was to come was important, and I hoped Raina was okay with the protection. As promised, Julian arrived within the hour at my parents dock, and Christopher and Michael escorted us down. Julian gave the coordinates to where we would be, in the event they did not hear back from us in the morning. My parents held no resistance to us leaving amidst the turmoil, and thanked Julian for taking care of me.

"Sandy, don't thank me. I'm glad I am here for this. I can't imagine you dealing with this alone. It will be fine. This is just an adjustment, and there's a lot of excitement. Like the sheriff said, it's about to get a lot worse. The best we can do is to make it as normal as possible for us all," Julian said comfortingly.

My father shook his hand and waved us off into the night. Once into the main channel, Julian hit the waves much harder, since the waters were choppier than before. I gripped the side of the seat to keep from bouncing each time the bow slammed down. We reached the cove shortly thereafter. Julian went into the cabin and brought back a small cooler. "We need to sleep down below tonight since it's supposed to rain, but we can stay out here as long as you want."

He handed me a bottle of water and asked if I was hungry. Feeling famished, I removed a few plastic containers of fresh fruit, chicken salad, and potato chips. We didn't bother with plates, and used plastic forks to share the food.

"Thanks for bringing me out here, and for everything today. It's just all so crazy. I can't imagine most people with amnesia deal with this. I mean, they have to go through the process of knowing who they were and whatnot, but having the place they live go into lockdown? It's so surreal."

Julian took a sip of his water and set the container of fruit down next to him. "Your situation is definitely unique. Even as a doctor, I constantly have to gauge the best way to react. But I have to be your friend first. And as a soldier, that adds a whole new level of emotion to this."

I laughed and grabbed the fruit. "But you're kind of the perfect person to be dealing with this right now. I can't think of anyone else that would have stayed so calm."

Julian huffed. "I am not really calm right now. I know you need me to keep it together."

"Well, after tomorrow you can leave me in the hands of the team. You won't have to worry about me so much. I won't be going back to the bakery." I was saddened by the thought of not helping in the morning, but I knew it would cause too much trouble.

"You can still come; you just can't bus tables and take orders anymore. I don't know how much fun you will have cooking all day, but I refuse to make you stop having a life because others want to hound you. Nothing should ever stop you from going anywhere; you just have to be a little more conscious how things happen," he said.

Feeling my sadness, he patted my thigh before standing. "I have a surprise for you tomorrow. I know you will love it, but first I think we need to get to sleep. It's really late, or should I say early, and we don't want to lose a day. Go down and change, and I will be there in a bit."

I liked surprises and smiled. "You've already seen me naked, why so shy?"

Julian shot me a look not to test him, but grinned right back. "You are trouble, Miss Brady."

I laughed and walked down into the cabin with my bag. I ducked my head at the bottom of the stairs, and was a bit shocked how spacious it was below. Touching the soft cotton blanket on the bed with my fingers, I felt my body flood with warmth. Julian and I were completely alone. His alpha behavior earlier in the day only stoked the fires burning deep. Without hesitation, he stepped forward to direct my protection. Lost in thought, I did not hear him walk down the steps. Only the deep inhalation of breath announced his arrival.

Wearing just a bra and panties, nearly every inch of my skin and ink was vulnerable to his gaze. I held my waist at first to hide my body, then met him eye to eye before allowing my arms to slack.

"It's okay to look," I said, the words rolling lazily off my tongue.

Reaching behind my back, my fingers loosened the snaps on my bra and let it drop to the floor. The pace of Julian's breath increased as I slowly approached him. For the first time in months, I was feeling . . . dare I say, adventurous.

"Stella . . ."

I smiled and placed my hand behind his head, dragging my nails lightly down his neck and over his chest. "Close your eyes, Julian."

I watched as his lids flickered, with long lashes brushing against his strong cheekbones. Without asking, I leaned up and brushed my lips across his. His body stood frozen, unmoved by my brazen attempts.

"What are you doing?" He groaned.

I brought my lips to his ear, opened my mouth, and let the warm air caress the shell, before curling my lips into a smile. "Exerting my independence."

Chapter 12

~ History Repeats Itself ~

Julian laughed at my boldness. My attempts to be a seductress fell upon a well-seasoned soldier.

"Why are you laughing at me? Do you find this funny?"

He shook his head and brought his lips closer to my mouth. "No, I find this ironic."

"How so?" I asked with a pout.

He responded with the same lightheartedness. "Because this is the same thing you did the first night we were together. You had me come out here to the cove and you tried to seduce me."

"Did it work?"

His pupils dilated while his hand trailed down my waist. "Of course it did. I was an eighteen-year-old boy, hopelessly in love with you."

I giggled and allowed my lips to meet the soft curve of his neck. "Will you indulge me once more then?"

Reaching down to grab his hand, I brought it to my breast and squeezed over his fingers.

Julian's head tilted back and he exhaled loudly.

"Tell me how it happened. How did I lose my innocence?"

My wording caused a moment of hesitancy, yet did not stop his eyes from devouring my body. He bent down and gently lifted me up. With my legs cradled in the crook of his arm, I smiled while being carried the short distance to the bed. When he set me down, I tried to scoot toward the headboard, but his fingers grabbed my hips and held them in place.

His eyes found mine and they were dark and full of need. "I am not going to tell you, Stella. I want to show you."

I watched anxiously as his hands moved over my bare stomach and thighs. Soft lips brushed down my legs, followed by gentle bites. "I love this piece," he said.

I looked down and watched his face as he traced the tattoo along my upper thigh with his fingers and a broad smile.

"Why?" I asked curiously.

Julian tilted his head and started at the bottom of the tattoo, which was near the back of my knee.

"This is the life cycle of a vine, and the harvest. Only someone who has seen it first-hand could know to ask for such important details. The type of leaves, the color and shape of the fruit, the pruning. These are my grapes, I know them well. But most importantly, I know it meant something to you, and you thought of me after you vanished."

I looked at the design once more with new understanding. "Why do I feel like all of my tattoos have something to do with you?"

Shaking his head, his eyes found the Venus flytrap. But he would not touch it. "I can see where some might, but I don't think that one does, especially considering its placement."

Intrigued by his analysis, I asked him to explain further. Although the stories sidetracked from my original intention, I relished in being so intimate with Julian while discovering more about who I was.

"Well," he said, "across your hipbone, you have a large cluster of grapes ready to be cut. The next step would be to press them. I used to tell you that your taste was sweeter than any grape I had ever tried, and got me drunker than any wine on earth ever could. If that is why you chose to do the tattoo this way, I would imagine the other is a form of warning."

I shivered thinking about anyone touching me but him. That part of my past was one I was curious about, but without truly knowing who I had been with, I had to contend with the present. I didn't want to think about those things. I only wanted to focus on Julian.

"So apparently, for the most part, I loved you so much I made my body a walking shrine of devotion. I would say that is kind of weird, but sweet, like when Van Gogh cut off his ear."

Julian laughed and leaned up to remove his shirt. The breath caught in my throat—not at how incredibly hard muscled and perfect he was beneath the thin piece of cotton, but that he had his own memorial dedicated to me in ink, though not nearly as elaborate. On the left side of his chest, over his heart, was a simple keyhole. On my left wrist was a key that matched perfectly. He lay on his side, reached for my hand, placed it over the tattoo, and exhaled deeply.

"I would have cut off my ear for you. I would have done anything for you. Losing you nearly killed me, and I know what it's like to almost die," he said softly.

I closed my eyes, thinking about the breath being stolen from his lungs.

"I know about the IED. Your mom told me. I am so glad you are alive. If it happened and I discovered you didn't live, I know it would have been so much harder for me to cope. I don't want to think about a life without you in it."

Julian brushed the short hairs across my forehead. "Sssshhhh . . . you are supposed to be seducing me right now. What happened with that?"

I raised my brows and giggled. "I believe you were going to show me how good of a job I was doing."

Giving a mischievous grin, Julian sat up and shifted my hips. Slowly, his hands ran up and down my body, before he pried my shaking legs apart. I gasped when his lips grazed my skin and began to give intermittent licks along my thighs, keeping his eyes locked on mine until he made his way down to the most intimate part of me. I cried out the moment his tongue hit my center, and he worked fastidiously to bring me pleasure. I was unable to keep my eyes open, and melted against the mattress. Gripping the sheets, his shoulders, anywhere I could place my hands to find a balance, I felt myself mentally falling apart beneath him.

I allowed my labored breathing to subside, and Julian's

lips danced back up along the center of my torso, onto my neck, and back to my mouth.

"Does this feel good?" he asked.

"This is incredible," I squealed delightfully.

Now rested between my legs, I could feel his erection through the rough denim of his jeans pressing painfully into my swollen crest.

"Kiss me Julian," I begged.

He leaned down, and his lips met mine tentatively. I pulled back and looked to him for answers. He rolled away and started to remove his pants. Standing at the edge of the bed, he seemed unsure if he should get back in. There was no way I was letting him change his mind, now that I had an idea of what was possible. I crawled onto my knees, and leaned up to where he stood. My lips pressed gently against his sternum, while my hand explored over his trunks. I felt his cock twitch in my palm as I slowly moved across the thin fabric, then I noticed his chest jerk momentarily. I looked up at him with a playful smile, seeking confirmation that I could proceed.

His hand gently massaged the back of my neck as I slid my fingers slowly along the thick band of the trunks and felt the soft skin of his abdomen. I gently rolled the fabric down, wanting to savor this moment as long as I could. Although I knew in my mind I had been with him before, I couldn't remember it. These memories were fresh, and would be mine alone. I closed my eyes and smelled his skin, licking the hollows of his abdomen, and tasting the saltiness on my tongue. Julian took incredible care of his body, and I wanted to devour every inch of it. He stepped back and pulled the trunks down, then kicked them to the side. My eyes darted to the rock-hard extension proudly raised to the sky. Pursing my lips in approval, I raised my right hand to my brow and gave a salute.

"Did you just salute my dick?" he asked in a half-humored tone.

"Isn't that what you are supposed to do when you want to show respect?" I giggled.

Julian shook his head and stood in front of me again, moving his palm up and down slowly along his length. I was unable to tear my eyes away, and immediately wanted to know how it would feel in my own hands. I could see a small droplet form at the top, which he wiped away with this thumb. He reached out with his other hand, and brought mine up to replace his and mimic the smooth strokes. He showed me how much pressure he liked, and how fast he wanted me to go. Another droplet formed and I couldn't contain the urge to know what it tasted like. I dropped my head, took him into my mouth, and gently sucked.

"Fuck," Julian yelped.

I jerked away in fear that I hurt him somehow. I wiped my mouth with the back of my hand, and apologized.

"I'm sorry, I didn't mean to . . ." I choked out.

Julian pulled me back up and held both sides of my face to look at him. "No, no, baby. I just wasn't expecting that. You didn't do anything wrong. I am just surprised, in a good way. I haven't been with anyone in a really long time, and I want this to be about you. I don't want you disappointed."

He could tell I was confused.

"Why would I be disappointed?"

Julian laughed and rubbed his brow, trying to

determine the best way to explain. "Honestly, Stella, if we do this, I won't last very long the first time. I know the moment I feel you, it will probably be over within seconds. But after that, it's on."

I smiled and wondered aloud. "Did that happen the first time, too?"

He turned a slight shade of red, and I was thankful he found this conversation funny.

"Actually, it did. But I more than made up for it, just like I will tonight if you let me," he said sincerely.

"Then what are you waiting for?" I pounced up excitedly, but he looked around the boat and seemed frustrated.

"I don't exactly have what I need here. I wasn't expecting this. We can go back out, but I doubt anything is open, and I don't have any at the house. Fuck!" Julian lightly hit the wall and banged his head a few times. He turned back to see me sitting completely naked on the bed, waiting with a huge smile on my face, and he didn't share my sense of mirth.

I crawled off the bed and reached for my purse, then pulled out a small box of condoms and walked over to him proudly. "You don't need these, but I got them just in case they would make you feel better."

"Why don't we need them?" Julian asked, puzzled, while holding the box tightly.

"Haven't you looked at my charts? Apparently I had an IUD placed a few months before my accident. They left it in. I have to check the strings, which feel like fishing wire, so I hope they don't poke you or anything."

I went to keep rambling, and Julian stopped me with

his finger across my lips. "Stella, it's really okay. It won't feel like that. Thank you for your concern, and yes, I have seen your charts, and I did know. I just forgot. This wasn't something I thought would happen, so I paid little attention to those parts of your health history. And as much as I love talking about you and medicine, my lips would be better served doing other things."

My heart instantly sped up as our mouths collided. Falling back onto the bed, I savored the weight of him pressing down onto me. With one arm balancing his body weight to the side, the other reached down and grabbed his cock, then slid the head gently up and down, teasing my entrance. It felt as though I truly had a Venus flytrap, and I wanted to snare him between my legs. I moaned impatiently, and in return, he smiled against my neck.

"Say my name, Stella."

"Julian." I sighed.

I felt the tip enter a bit then withdraw, causing me to whine in protest.

"Say it again, Stella."

Breathlessly I huffed out, "Julian."

I quickly realized what he wanted, and began to chant his name over and over again as he sank his hips and filled my body. His full weight pressed into me, while he grappled with restraint. Unconsciously, my channel clenched around the unfamiliar presence.

"Stop it." He laughed.

"I can't! My vagina has a mind of its own."

Julian leaned back up on propped elbows and hovered over my face. I lifted my head to kiss his nose and smiled sweetly. For the first time since we found one another again, his face was fully relaxed. There was not one line of worry or concern.

"What are you thinking about?" I asked him.

He frowned slightly turned his head away. "About us. The future. What will happen?"

Sadness trailed his words.

I reached up and brought his gaze back to mine. "Stay with me, Julian. Don't think about later."

Realizing the propensity we both held for thinking the worst, he brought his focus back and twisted his hips. I cried out his name, and locked my ankles around his waist to pull him closer. He instructed me to drop my legs, gently pressed them back, and rested my calves against his shoulders.

"Tell me if this is too much, Stella," he said while sliding in slowly.

My eyes rolled into the back of my head, and I moaned loudly. I couldn't stop the noises from leaving my chest each time I felt him move deeper. With each intake of air, I exhaled his name. Our skin began to grow warm, with a thin sheen of sweat forming between us. The passion created an intoxicating aroma, and my mouth became parched from breathing so heavily. Every sensation my body was experiencing burned deeply into my consciousness. The way I felt small beneath Julian, so safe and protected, and how every skilled move of his hand was driven by memories of us. He knew exactly what to do to drive me to the unknown, and he held me tightly enough that I knew I could let go. With one final thrust, I screamed his name before feeling my body jerk uncontrollably as waves of warmth radiated through each limb. Through the fog, I heard him call out for me as he found his own release.

It was as if I left my body and connected with heaven, before crashing back down. Our bodies separated, and I felt a void of emptiness between us. I didn't want to need him this way. Curling into his chest, I let the tears fall. His arms encompassed my body, pulling me close and offering comfort through the myriad of complex emotions. I felt my eyelids grow heavy, but one last gift poured out of my heart. I leaned up and kissed the keyhole, then rested my palm over it. With sleepy words, I was unsure if he heard me. However, the tightened grip and kiss on my head told me he did.

"I love you, too," he replied.

With that, I had the anchor I needed to enter the darkness at peace. And I prayed to God it wouldn't be the last time.

Chapter 13

~ Surrender ~

The start of the engines roused me from a deep slumber. Unsure if the night before really happened, or was just a lucid dream, I sat up to rub my eyes and felt the strain in my muscles and tenderness between my legs. It had most definitely happened, and the realization caused me to smile. The only feeling I could remember that surpassed it, was the rush of pounding against the road when I ran away from Julian. Laughing to myself, I rolled off the bed and rifled through my bag for the shorts and long sleeve shirt I packed. Several times I had to hold the wall for balance, as the boat skipped across waves at high speed. I grabbed the rails to the upper deck, made my way to the captain's chair, and wrapped my arms around Julian's waist from behind. Rather than sinking into my embrace, he pulled my arms away and turned around with a frigid stare. The man standing before me was not the same man who only hours earlier sent my body into an exquisite chaos.

"What's wrong, Julian," I shouted. I could tell that

something was definitely amiss, but for the second time, I chose to ignore it. Looking out onto the banks of the lake, I could see my parents' dock off in the distance.

He slowed the boat down, and finally decided to speak, but refused to look at me. "Last night was a mistake, Stella. It should have never happened." Julian's face dropped slightly as he forced the words out.

I waited for more to be said, but nothing else came. A million emotions collided in my brain, careened into my heart, and then settled in my stomach like a heavy rock. Parts of me wanted to sink into the ground and cry, but those parts were negligible judging by the speed at which my fingers curled into a ball and landed painfully against his perfectly-chiseled jaw. With eyes focused on the water, he wasn't expecting such a violent reaction, and was taken off guard. The boat was going slow enough not to veer into the banks, and Julian instinctively pulled back the throttle after hitting the side of the boat. He rubbed the sore spot with his hand and breathed deeply, yet remained silent.

Adrenaline was still coursing through my veins, and the punch only amplified my anger.

"People make mistakes all the time; it doesn't justify treating them like garbage. I am not a mistake!"

Before I could continue arguing, he pulled off to the side and killed the engine. "Stella, stop twisting my words! I said last night was a mistake. I never said you were. And I am not trying to treat you like garbage. I just can't do this, we can't do this. Everything will fall apart."

A flash of despair passed through his eyes the brief moment they met mine.

I closed my eyes as the tears fought through. I knew

the truth, even though I didn't want to admit it.

"It already is."

Feeling my heart crumble, I turned and focused on the boat slip where Michael was waiting with Truman. I was certain they could hear the argument across the water, and stood defensively. Julian traversed the short distance over, and the men approached to help me off the boat. They did not speak as they recognized the tension radiating off of my body. Looking to Julian with disdain, Truman stepped forward and used his foot to shove the boat away from the edge after helping me off. As long as I was in this frame of mind, and under their watch, Julian was not welcome without my request. I went straight to the bathroom, closed the door, and stripped bare. Then I filled the tub with steaming water and sunk neck deep. Only one thought crossed my mind as my skin began to flush. Ignorance really was bliss.

For nearly two hours, I poured fresh hot water into the bath as soon as it would cool. The large garden tub was surrounded by floor-to-ceiling windows looking out onto the lake. Set up on a polished granite platform, the copper faucets and fixtures created a rustic refuge I utilized often. Returning from her morning rounds, my mother gently tapped on the door before entering. I sank beneath the surface and listened to her feet quietly walk across the floor, then I heard the weight of her body hit the wooden chair next to me. Only able to hold my breath so long, my swollen eyes could not stay hidden forever.

"What happened?" she asked softly.

I pursed my lips and stared out onto the lake. "I don't want to talk about it. Besides, you said that certain things need to stay between Julian and me."

My mother gasped lightly, and brought her hand to her mouth. Several minutes went by before either of us spoke again. My statement, although evasive, was clear as to the source of my distress. I knew she was trying to process how the situation even presented itself. It doesn't take a scientist to figure out what happens when you place two people alone in a highly-charged situation when there is already tension. Like two magnets drawn together by universal law, suddenly we were repelled by equal force, skyrocketing in opposite directions.

"Oh Stella . . . why would you put yourself in that position?" she asked.

I laughed and shrugged my shoulders. "I will tell you the same thing I told him. I was exerting my independence. I am not a child, and I can't stay in this bubble forever. I have to live as though my memory isn't coming back, and if I am to do that to the fullest, why should I be exempt from falling in love?"

She caught sight of the tears that slipped from my eyes before I was able to wipe them away. She stood up from the chair, pulled my wet body tight to hers, and cried with me. How do you argue with that? Does a disability, whether physical or mental, mean that a person is less human? That they shouldn't have every opportunity to experience the most basic of all primal needs, to love and be loved in return? Like the appearance of the press, this was another unexpected turn of events.

"It's so complicated, Stella; it's not that easy, especially for you two."

Lying docilely in her arms, I shook my head in disagreement. "No, it's not really. It's a choice. And he made it. I cannot change the way his emotions are choosing to rule, any more than I can change mine. He tried telling me that this is just all one biological cocktail, and maybe it is. But last night . . . last night was so much more than logic and reason. I know what I felt, what I feel. And maybe that makes me a complete moron, but I am not sorry. The only thing I will apologize for is how my actions affect you and dad."

She smoothed my hair away from my face, and kissed the top of my forehead. With a bright smile that reached her eyes, she nodded her head. "Stella, you are a grown woman, and you are right—shame on him. Although I wouldn't have expected you two to hook up so soon, I know things happen. I cannot answer for his behavior, or tell you what you should do next. What I can say is this: do not ever feel bad or guilty for falling in love. That doesn't mean the other person will reciprocate, but that is never a guarantee, only a hope. Also know when to walk away. You are worth so much more than someone who cannot face his own feelings when it comes to you. I love Julian, I really do. But you are first and foremost my daughter, and I want only the best. I am so sorry you have to learn this the hard way. But that is the price of being a Brady. You are a stubborn bunch."

I laughed for the first time that afternoon, and then pulled the plug in the tepid water. My fingers were deeply wrinkled, and I felt a bit light headed from dehydration. My mother handed me a large fluffy towel and helped me down the steps. I watched as her eye caught the tattoo on my hip, and she smirked. Pulling the thick cotton aside, I showed her again and wiggled.

"I think a little bit more of who you are is coming out every day." She snickered.

Tracing the green and violet carnivorous plant with my fingers, I looked up and smiled.

"You know, the guys told me I wasn't a bad person. Most of this was a defense mechanism I hid behind. Now that I am learning more about who I was, I can understand my reluctance to vulnerability. Maybe that is what this is all about. God didn't want me living a life of fear. If people believed I was this angry and destructive woman, they wouldn't get close enough to break my heart. It's kind of the same thing now, isn't it?"

While waiting for my mother's response, I could see she was debating between words of comfort and honesty. Thankfully, she found a way to convey both. "Unfortunately, it is. However, it is like you said—a choice how you respond. If you believe God want's something better for you, you are absolutely right. He uses everything good and bad to bring us closer to Him. It is not us who should be teaching you how to live, I think it's the opposite. All of us have something we need to learn from you. We forget what it is like to have nothing to lose, and to live without fear. I admire your bravery, banged knees and all."

I hugged her and started to walk down the hallway to my bedroom, then I turned around and gave her a mischievous smile. "Depending on the circumstance, it's always worth getting a little banged up."

With wide eyes she threw the towel at me and shrieked. "Stella Elizabeth Brady! If your father heard what you just said, we would both be in the dog house!"

I shrugged and went back toward my bedroom before I heard her call again. "Stella."

"Yes, mama."

With a wink and a smile she quietly agreed. "Good for you."

I felt lighter entering the cool bedroom with the shades drawn, blocking the afternoon sun from forming a sauna. Digging through the drawers for a pair of clean undies, my fingers grazed a piece of folded paper. I pulled it out, and my breathing increased. I'd forgotten I had shoved the article to the bottom of the drawer. I opened it up, and scanned the images on the cover. I instantly gravitated toward the picture of the man. He was beautiful. Different than Julian in so many ways, but he was someone else who knew me. If Julian felt that this path was a mistake, perhaps this one would feel differently. There was only one way to find out.

Chapter 14

~ Summoned ~

For the millionth time, it seemed I soaked in every word printed on the thin newspaper. "Stella Brady Tragedy" was in bold black print. Below it was a photo of me and the subheading: "Paparazzi chase leaves lead singer of Protest in critical condition, her companion shaken."

My companion.

His name was Kai Bennett, drummer for the band Mistaken Identity. *Who was this man to me?*

At 10:45 this morning, Stella Brady was injured on the Portuguese Gap ski run while being pursued by Los Angeles based photographer Richard Sabatalo in Park City, Utah. She is listed in critical condition at Park City Medical and no additional information has been provided. The singer was in town for the annual film festival, and was scheduled to begin a cross country tour at the end of the month. All shows have been cancelled until further notice. Mr. Bennett's publicist has released a statement on his behalf, expressing distress over the day's events and a desire for privacy during this time.

The article went on to explain more about who I was, including my rise to stardom and journey with the band Protest. I was discovered in Nashville by the daughter of a record producer, who convinced her father to listen to an unassuming bartender that had never stepped foot inside a studio. Within a year, we released our debut album, and the sky was the limit. The rapid ascension was not without consequence. It was rumored I was troubled, with drug use and erratic behavior. I was warned not to read too much into what the media said about me, that most of it was speculation dusted with fact. One thing that could not be disputed was that Kai Bennett was with me when the accident occurred, and only he could answer the questions that haunted my dreams.

The unknowing became unbearable, and finally, I could take it no more. My parents left for dinner that evening, and I stayed behind to speak to Michael and place my request. I needed to talk to Kai, and he was my best chance of that happening. He was initially cautious, so I explained my plight.

Agreeing it might be beneficial, he recommended a few precautions be taken before the introduction occurred. "Stella, it's not that simple, but it's not impossible. Mr. Bennett must agree to a nondisclosure of anything that is said between you two. Your condition is not public knowledge, and we must do everything we can to protect it. Based off what I know about Kai, I don't see that being an issue. I remember how upset he was when you got hurt."

Imagining being in Kai's shoes caused my chest to tighten. Perhaps it was the sting of rejection driving me toward him. Regardless of the reason, he held answers I desperately needed. Several weeks passed before Michael was able to connect with Kai and arrange his travel. Julian had stayed away, and my parents did not press the issue. I spent my days working in the garden, painting, and learning how to use the computer more. For as much as I wanted to read more about who I was, I cleared the browser every time I typed my name. I also gave myself the opportunity to be surprised, and refrained from looking up anything about Kai. I wanted to be free of judgment and assumption. Excitedly, I passed my time thinking of all the things I would ask him. Thinking back to the conversation with my mother in the bathroom, I decided that until Kai arrived, I needed to make things right with my fathers, both heavenly and here on earth. Sunday morning rolled around and I dressed the most conservative I was able to with the clothing in my possession. Christopher chose to join me, and he too put on his nicest suit.

We were the last to arrive, and walked quietly into the small church. My father sat in a pew to the side of the altar, reserved for lecturers and elders. Everyone turned when the heavy wooden doors closed behind us, but we paid no attention as we found our seats. I watched my father like a hawk, and he watched me in return, wondering what would happen during the hour of service. After the homily, the congregation began to sing hymns of praise. They happened to choose one of my favorite songs, that I felt I hadn't heard in forever. Closing my eyes, I lost myself in worship, leaving all of my worries behind. Having Christopher with me set my heart at ease. He did not mind one bit when I held his hand and leaned against his arm, praying for God to lead me through this valley. He had tissues ready, anticipating the tears that would come.

It was not until he squeezed my hand hard that I pulled out of the fog. I must have continued to sing long after everyone had stopped. Embarrassed, I sat down and tried to keep from hyperventilating. I looked up toward the front, and anticipated a look of horror on my father's face. If I had been such a disappointment, I could only imagine what this would have done to him. Rather than a face full of disdain, his eyes were reddened and holding back tears. A large smile rested broadly on his cheeks. He was not ashamed of my presence. He was proud. I kept quiet during the rest of the service, daring not to sing another note, but beaming with hope that things may just right themselves in my world somehow.

After the dismissal, I waited for the congregation to leave and greet the pastor as they headed out for the day. Feeling infinitely lighter, I tapped my head against Christopher once more and giggled. "Thank you for being here today, it means a lot."

He bumped my arm in return and laughed. "Stella, this is a side of you no one has ever gotten to see. I understand now how those pipes became so fine tuned. You truly have a gift. It was an honor for me to be here."

I smiled and stood, ready to leave and speak with my father. He was standing next to Pastor Williams, and smiled brightly as I approached. I only knew the pastor by name via conversations overheard during dinner. Up until this moment, I had never met the man. He too held the look of fondness so many had, bringing me ease in the unfamiliar situation. My father grabbed me and held me close, shaking slightly. My presence here was the key to breaking down his walls. I felt it in his embrace, that any resentment or anger he held was melted away on the steps of the church. He looked up to Christopher, reached out his hand, and thanked him for coming. Only afterward, did he offer a formal introduction between the pastor and I.

Pastor Williams was around the same age as my father. A head of salt and pepper hair rested against a cleanly-shaven face and crisp white color so common of clergy. He reached out to take my hand, and I thanked him for the beautiful service.

"Stella, you used to sing here. For many years, your voice blessed these walls. I never thought I would hear it again, so it's me that wants to thank you. I know you have been in town for a while, and I was hoping you would eventually find your way here. God must have heard me, because here you are," he said.

More pieces of the puzzle began to fall in place. Outside of Julian, I still had my own life here. But why wouldn't I? Of course there was more to my past than the one I shared with Julian. The more I learned about the life I vanished from, the more intrigued I became with what caused me to disappear. I had a good life, I was loved, and had anything I could ever possibly hope for. What happened? Knowing Kai would be arriving in a few short hours kept me distracted enough from that which I may never know. I said my goodbyes to Pastor Williams and my father, hopping excitedly into the SUV for my reintroduction to Kai Bennett.

For weeks, I had studied the image of his face on the

newspaper clipping. Another photo showed him on stage playing the drums, but from a further distance. Like me, long limbs were decorated in vibrant ink images. His hair was a dirty blond in both images, and his eyes were ocean blue, so familiar yet so hard to place. In the full-bodied picture, he was shirtless, tan, and built of rippling hard muscle. I patted myself on the back and laughed. At least I knew how to pick attractive men. Thinking about him being at my house when I arrived made me nervous to the point of nausea. Questions swarmed through my mind. *What if he didn't like me? What if I meant nothing to him? Why did he agree to come down here? Would he tell everyone how messed up I was?*

I banged my head against the back of the seat, so Christopher reached out and grabbed my hand.

"Stella, everything will be fine. I am right here," he stated calmly.

"I didn't tell you what was bothering me."

Christopher squeezed my hand harder. "You didn't need to, I already know. And I am saying it will be fine."

I squeezed back and snuggled up next to the giant man. I felt as though, next to him, nothing would or could ever hurt me. I had amazing people that took care of me; I shouldn't have worried as much as I did. Pulling up to the house, I could see another vehicle parked in the driveway. Michael was sitting outside on the porch waiting to greet us, and walked down to open the car door. Stepping out, I looked around in confusion.

"Where is he?" I asked, anticipating he would be on the porch waiting for my arrival.

"He went for a walk. He's down at the lake with Truman. But Stella, he still doesn't know. Remember that.

There's no telling how he will react. We have no reason to believe you are in danger, just be careful."

I smiled at Michael and nodded my head, then I tuned toward the water, and bounded off excitedly in Kai's direction. *He's here. He's here.* It was almost too much to believe. At the edge of the tree line, I stopped just out of view. Taking a moment to observe at a distance, I soaked in every beautiful feature. His hair was shorter than the picture in the article, and smoothed down from wearing a ball cap that was resting next to him. His muscular arms were covered from wrist, up, in colorful tattoos, and I could see more peeking through the V-neck of his T-shirt, as well as up the back collar line. His khaki jeans were rolled up to his calves, while his long legs moved back and forth in the cool water. He would look up the hill every few moments, waiting to see me cross the path onto the dock, so finally I walked slowly toward him.

Kai turned and looked right at my short hair, before coming back to my eyes, but the beautiful smile never left his face. When he moved to stand up, I was taken aback by his height. At nearly Christopher's height, he was a bit intimidating. I stopped a few feet in front of him, unsure of what to do or say, so I began with the only thing I could think of.

"Hi." I giggled. It sounded so inadequate for such a momentous occasion.

Kai moved toward me and tilted his head. "Hi to you." He laughed.

The summer sun had warmed his skin, and I could smell the sumptuous cologne radiating from his body. I closed my eyes and let the breeze carry it over to me, then felt my head begin to spin.

"I can't believe you are really here," I whispered.

A soft hand grazed my cheek, catching me off guard and creating an involuntary shudder.

"Fuck, I'm sorry Stella. It's just . . . I never thought I would see you again. You have no idea how badly I want to grab you right now and never let go. I had to touch you just to know you are real."

After a moment of contemplation, I stepped forward and tentatively wrapped my arms around Kai's waist, while pressing my face against his chest. I could feel his heart beating so hard, the pace nearly matched his rapid breathing. Strong arms embraced my shoulders as he tucked his chin over my head and held firmly.

"I'm really here, but I have to tell you something." I stepped back and felt the frown pulling the edges of my lips down against my will.

Looking concerned, he took a deep breath and waited for me to speak.

"Kai. I appreciate you coming down here, you have no idea how much. But the accident did a lot of damage. I am sorry, but I don't remember you. You look really familiar, but the only reason I know who you are is because of a newspaper article I found by chance. I was hoping you could help me answer a few questions."

I prepared for him to recoil, but he merely tilted his head again and brought his hand to his mouth, thinking deeply about the words I had just spoken. After a few moments, he threaded his fingers behind his neck, and rocked back and forth on his heels calmly, and exhaled a deep breath. My eyes began to burn with tears of rejection, but before the first one fell, Kai gave a crooked smile and reached his hand out to mine. I slid my fingers against his rough palms, and he quickly embraced them, pulling me back into his arms.

"Ask me anything you want, and I will answer as best as I can. But I have something to tell you. I don't know you that well, either," he said quietly.

I paused and met his gaze, which was filled with so much love and light. He looked at me differently than Julian. I felt as if this man adored me. Was he infatuated with the star I was, or was he intimate with the woman off stage? I pressed my nose into his chest, and could feel the heat of my breath curl into the cotton fabric of his shirt as I spoke. "Please tell me what you know."

Kai's hand began to rub gently up and down along my spine, encouraging me to stay close. "I was obviously with you during the accident, but I had only really met you the night before. Your manager was on our bus partying, and promised I would get to meet you if I came with her. She dragged along some groupie, but I knew who you were and it was the only chance I had. You stay pretty guarded. So I went, and I waited, and surely enough, you came and crawled into bed with me. I couldn't believe my luck. At first you wouldn't have anything to do with me, you were just messing around with Vida. But when you realized I'd waited for you, you took me back to your room and. . . ."

My body froze thinking about what happened next. I knew he wouldn't tell me unless I asked, but I had come too far to not know exactly what events took place before my demise.

"And?" I whispered.

"And we did it, ya know? It was out of this world, crazy. Then we went snowboarding, and you had some blow, so we got high before going down the run. Your nose started bleeding, and there was this photographer . . ."

I grabbed my head and walked away shaking. Kai was a one night stand. I didn't know him. He was a complete stranger. Why was I so drawn to him, when clearly nothing good came out of us meeting? I was so foolish. He moved quickly and placed his hands gently on my shoulders.

"Stella, I am sorry. I wish I didn't have to tell you that. I wish more than anything I meant something to you. That's why I came, because I thought I actually did. It wasn't your fault what happened. You were trying to get away. You actually tried to leave me behind, but I wouldn't let you. I heard you cry out my name before you hit the tree. It was the most horrible thing I had ever heard or seen in my entire life. I rushed over to you and you wouldn't move. There was so much blood. I just held you close and asked God to not let you die. I told Him I would get sober, do anything, just not to let you die. And I did. I got sober. Because of you."

Kai's eyes were red, and his skin grew blotchy. This was obviously an emotional situation for him as well. It was impossible for me to know how it traumatized him. It made me feel a little better to know something else good came out of it. I smiled and this time I was the one to reach out my hand to him and pull him close, the magnet in my heart drawing me into him.

"She likes you."

He looked at me in confusion.

"She?"

"Yes, the person I became. I have no recollection of that life, so it's easier for me to refer to her in third person.

I feel like I have a ghost living in my body, and I know it's her fighting to come back. It's not like schizophrenia, it's more like a knowing. When I first saw your pictures, I felt this warmth spread through my body. I tingled all the way to my toes, and my heart beat so hard. I knew I had to meet you."

Kai smiled. "I am happy to be here, Stella. You have no idea. I feel like you are God's reward for going down the straight and narrow. You are a fucking miracle."

I laughed at his comment, and quite liked the idea of being someone's proof of a higher power.

"You believe in God, I take it?" I asked with a huge grin.

"That I do. We haven't always seen eye to eye, but He always manages to find a way to keep me steady."

Noticing that Kai's eyes kept moving to my mouth, I asked if I had something in my teeth.

He laughed loudly. "Um, no Stella. I'm sorry. I just can't stop thinking about kissing you, honestly."

My eyes grew wide and my stomach fluttered. Imagining his lips on mine caused my mouth to water in anticipation. The air between us grew tangible, and I could think of nothing else. I moved my chest closer to his, and felt my breath grow shaky. The moment his hand rested against my cheek, I melted into his palm and closed my eyes. I parted my lips slightly and waited for him to move. The air puffed out of his nostrils and his face moved closer to mine. He wrapped his other arm tightly around my waist and pulled me close. Time felt as though it was dragging along on purpose, just to torture me, until finally his lips brushed mine and offered sweet respite. A deep whine was pulled from my lungs, and I craved more as I tangled myself into him.

Kai's mouth crashed against mine, and his tongue greedily laid claim. He had been there before; not only because he told me, but because deep within I knew it. I craved him without knowing the source of my desire. I heard myself call out his name from a dark place, and he responded. With growls of satisfaction, I was consumed by him.

Stepping away, I breathed heavily and smiled. "Wow," was all I could muster.

Kai gave a smirk of approval and rubbed his belly. "Wow is right, but there is a more pressing matter. Airport food leaves a lot to be desired. Have you had dinner yet? It's getting late, and I am starving. Can we eat and then continue our conversation?"

I shook my head and laughed, while nodding toward the house.

"We have a stocked kitchen. I am sure we can find something, if that's okay. My parents are headed back, and I bet they will be hungry too."

Kai fell in step next to me, and grabbed my hand affectionately. "Anything you want, Stella."

Chapter 15

~ Reservations for Four ~

Kai began to assist me with the evening's meal without prompt. We shared stolen glances and titillating kisses, and I wasn't sure if I could let him leave. I shared my sentiment, and he looked far away.

"Stella, I would want nothing more than to stay here with you, but I have a tour to finish," he said sadly.

I nodded and brushed it off. "It was just a thought. I know it's impossible. I don't know you. Perhaps it's best if we get to know each other again from afar."

Kai's arms wrapped around me as his lips pressed firmly into the skin of my collarbone.

"You will get to know me; I will make damn sure of that. If you want me in your life, neither hell nor high water will stop that from happening."

I giggled and pressed my back into his chest. "I must have made quite the impression on you before."

He turned me around to face him, and pushed my body hard into the counter. "I've never been able to forget you. As hard as I tried, I couldn't wash myself of the memories. It sounds stupid, it was only one night, but that's all it took. No one will ever be able to take your place, Stella."

I wrapped my arms around his neck and pulled him closer for another searing kiss. I don't think I could ever tire of feeling his mouth against mine, and the way he dissolved all reason.

Hearing a surprised cough, I stopped and smirked. "Um, hi mom and dad . . . this is Kai. He was an old friend of mine. I hope you don't mind, he's staying for dinner. We're almost finished making it."

My father turned around and walked away, whereas my mother raised a cynical brow. Kai laughed while opening his arms and pulled my mother into a hug, lifting her up and spinning her around like a child. Once he sat her down, she held the side of his cheek and patted it affectionately.

"I wish I knew you were coming. This is quite the surprise."

Standing slack jawed at the scene which was unfolding, I waited until someone decided to enlighten me. Noticing my apprehension, I was rapidly growing more unsettled. Something about this picture was very wrong.

"How do you know him mom?"

They both turned to address me and their demeanors changed.

"Honey it's okay. I got to know Kai quite well at the hospital. He actually came along when we brought you here. Don't you remember?"

Flashes of the flight raced through my mind. The tall man in the black coat with the blue eyes.

"That was you?" I asked quietly.

I hadn't made the connection. His arms were covered and he was wearing glasses. By the time I had woken, he was already gone.

"Why didn't you guys tell me? Don't you think that's important?"

Feeling once again foolish, I stormed out the back door and leaned against the railing. Michael followed a few minutes behind and paused next me.

"Stella, we did not know about the hospital. I swear. He didn't tell us, neither did she. Everything was arranged through his manager. We did not have direct contact with Kai until he arrived at the airport, and would never knowingly have kept that from you. The moment you were admitted we were cut off from contact, you know that."

I smiled weakly and shrugged.

"I told her not to tell me things. This is why. The more I discover the worse it gets. I can't be angry at her for keeping it a secret. She knows how I react." I said with a laugh.

Looking into the house, I knew this was another day of revelation necessary for uncovering the truth. I wanted answers, and here they were. Just because I wasn't expecting this, didn't make it any less poignant. Giving myself a little longer to gather my thoughts, I opened the door slowly and my mother was standing next to Kai near the stove. They stopped talking and waited for me to speak.

"Perhaps now I can be included in the conversation." Inhaling the delicious aromas wafting from the pots placed me in a calmer mood and my own hunger was fueling my irritability. Giving a contrite smile, my mother stated she needed to freshen up and would be back shortly to set the table.

Kai let out a sigh of relief as she walked away and turned to me perplexed "You didn't tell them I was coming?" he asked nervously.

"No, I thought they would have discouraged it. This was one of those seek-forgiveness-rather-than-permission situations. Show's how much I really know. My life has been a train wreck since I was brought back here, especially once the paparazzi discovered my whereabouts. I live in a bubble. Literally," I said with disdain.

Approaching me confidently, I flinched when his fingers first grazed my skin but he was not moved. Without trepidation his caress lowered my guard.

"I know what you mean. I get it. It must be terrible to not remember who you were, when that's all the rest of the world sees. I wasn't sure how much she told you, I just assumed you knew. I'm sorry Stella."

I smiled and shook my head. "It's not your fault. I should apologize, that was out of line. Welcome to my life."

For the next half hour we moved about in a quiet comfort while getting dinner ready. Kai instructed me on how to slice the vegetables just so, and curl the lemon peels into small spirals. Each dish was painstakingly prepared and gorgeous. My mother returned just as we were putting the finishing touches on the first course.

Reluctantly, my father joined her, taking his place at the table and opening with a prayer. Unlike the dinner with Julian, I was not unsure of myself. I dismissed the curious glances of my parents as they watched the two of us interact. It was as natural as breathing, and I knew it frightened them.

I broke the tension with the only thing I knew that would get through to my father, who had not yet met Kai. "Kai believes in God, you know. He thinks I am a miracle." I joked between bites of sautéed shrimp.

My father's ears perked right up, and the investigation began. "Is that so? Tell me, what kind of religious upbringing you had?" he asked skeptically, while eyeballing the colorful palate adorning Kai's arms.

Kai winked at me before addressing him. "My dad is a preacher, as is my grandfather, and his father. I come from a long line of clergy. I feel as though the gift skipped me, as I never felt the call, but it doesn't mean that I don't know the bible inside and out."

I looked to my dad and raised my brows before taking another bite. The questions continued, yet each one came with a less cautious tone. My mother remained unusually quiet as I learned more about who Kai Bennett was, which did not go unnoticed by my father. He warmed up once the connection was made that Kai was the one that stayed vigilantly by my side until I awoke, which nearly cost him his career. Once my condition was diagnosed, Dr. Gleason and the neurology team at the hospital weighed out the risks of having him in my life, and the plans of my mother caring for me, it was deemed a complication in my recovery. If not for the article falling from the album, his presence in my life would have remained unknown. The end of the evening came far too quickly, and we were reminded he had a plane to catch.

Standing on the back porch, hot tears filled my eyes and poured down my cheeks. "I wish you didn't have to leave yet, but I am so grateful you agreed to see me. It's been such an amazing day."

Kai wiped my tears away and pulled me close. "Baby girl, I won't be gone long. We can always talk on the phone, or Skype. I know it's not the same, but I will come back here for you if you want me to. Just say the word, and I'm on my way."

My lips found his for one last kiss. I could taste the reluctance of our separation through the urgency in which he pressed against me and held me close. I whimpered as I tangled my arms around his neck, and with one arm tightly around my waist, he began to tickle my sides lightly to ease the sadness. I tossed my head back while laughing hysterically to escape his embrace just as headlights turned into the driveway and illuminated our bodies.

Recognizing the grill of Julian's truck, I froze in place. "Lovely."

"Who is that?" Kai asked as he continued to hold me close.

The wheels suddenly began to spin backward as Julian hit the gas, shooting gravel in every direction.

I tried to run toward the truck screaming his name, but it was too late. My parents heard the commotion and rushed to my side, as I picked up a handful of rocks and threw it into the cloud of dust.

Kai tried to come near me, but my father stopped him. "I think it's time for you to go son," he said.

Michael and Christopher were waiting to take him back

to the airport, and had opened the back door to the SUV.

"Wait!" I shouted.

Kai turned around with the most defeated expression on his face. I ran to him and jumped into his arms, tightening my legs around his waist. "Don't let me go," I whispered into his ear.

"Never."

I lowered to the ground and struggled to release him. After watching him step hesitantly into the car, I turned and ran into my bedroom, falling face first into pillows and screaming at the top of my lungs. The sound was muffled, but not enough to stop my mother from banging on the door.

"Stella Brady, you let me in this instant! What the hell were you doing, asking that boy to come here and acting the way you did? You can't do that! We are already dealing with enough, we don't need this."

"Excuse me? You let a man stay by my side and nearly lose everything, only to shut him out the moment I wake up and then act like nothing is wrong? I am not the selfish one here! You think you are protecting me but you aren't. This bubble has popped and no matter how much you try to keep me from the truth, it's like dad said, it's going to come out." My words were angry and cut deep. She sensed what was already going through my mind and knew there was no turning back. I resolved to find my way out of this town first thing in the morning. If I was such a burden, surely I had enough money to find some other place to live in anonymity and not upset others' lives. The thought of leaving my mother and father broke my heart, but the reality was I had been a tornado once before, and even amnesia couldn't keep that part of me at bay.

Chapter 16

~ Consequences ~

"Stella Brady, you get your ass up and dressed right now!"

The pounding on the door coincided with the ringing in my ears. Crying so hard had worn me down to nothing, and every sound was amplified infinitely. I needed water, but was too tired to move. A full day had passed and I was left uninterrupted to mourn, but now my mother was on a mission. I cracked the door and she stormed in, opening the shades and flooding the room with the bright afternoon sun.

"You smell like death. Take a shower first, we don't have much time, Raina is waiting," she said sternly.

"Why is Raina waiting for me?" I asked groggily while pulling clothes from the closet with a continuous yawn.

My mother walked past me into the bathroom, and turned the knobs to the shower, urging me to move faster.

"Because we aren't going to deal with this petty

nonsense between you two. You don't have to get along, but I refuse to let Raina take on any more stress than she needs. She has something to tell you, and you are going to listen. Do you hear me?"

I nodded softly and crawled under the steaming hot water. I wanted to savor it, but I heard my mother banging around angrily, so I washed up quickly to get on our way. My head was killing me and I still needed water, but with the mood she was in, I dared not ask. We turned out of the driveway, and rather than heading toward Mrs. Moreau's property, we headed into the city.

"Where are we going?" I asked curiously.

Sandy never took her eyes off the wheel and answered curtly. "She's getting a treatment today. She will be at the center for a few hours, so I am dropping you off and will pick you both up later."

I nodded quietly and stepped out of the truck at the entrance of the oncology building. With a small piece of paper guiding me to the room, I followed the instructions and quietly found a place next to Raina. She was asleep, so I didn't wake her, but it wasn't long before her frail hand reached out for mine.

"Stella, sweetheart, thank you for coming," she said softly.

"I really didn't have a choice, but I am happy to be here. I am sorry I've been away for so long, it's just . . ."

Raina put up her hand to hush me. "Stella, I know everything. I understand."

My eyes grew wide and I breathed a sigh of relief. "Thank you, Raina. I was beginning to feel like I was crazy for being upset."

Her eyes grew determined and somewhat distant, which indicated to me I shouldn't be so elated.

Several moments passed before she began to speak. "I may understand, but it does not mean I agree. There's something very important you need to know that I think might shed some light on this situation. My son refuses to tell you, but I will not hold back. This is bullshit. Complete and utter bullshit. You both do not have much time, and you need to work this out now while you can."

Raina began to cough profusely, alerting the technicians. They brought her water and insisted she relax, because it wasn't good for her to be so upset. I lowered my head while rubbing my hands together anxiously. I looked at her with a loss for words. I didn't know how to fix this.

"What can I possibly do? He want's nothing to do with me. He made that very clear."

My eyes began to sting thinking about how hurt I was that morning on the boat, feeling him push me away after giving myself to him.

Raina shook her head and looked off into the distance. "How was he supposed to feel when he was holding you in his arms, and as you slept, you cried out another man's name? And then, when he finally felt he could talk about it, he goes to see you and who does he find you with?" Her eyes met mine and I felt my stomach twist into a million knots.

"What are you talking about?" I cried.

Tears pooled in Raina's eyes and down her face. "Julian told me you were having a bad dream that night on the boat. He was unable to wake you because you were sleeping so deeply. You let out a blood curdling scream, and shouted out for Kai."

I shifted out of the chair and stood against the wall. "Impossible. How could I not remember that? Why wouldn't he tell me?" I began shaking and feeling dizzy. The anxiety made me feel like my body was in an iron vice, slowly tightening, squeezing out every breath.

"Because he knows where you are, and he is unable to save you. Don't you see? Julian is being forced to relive his worst nightmare."

I began to grow livid that no one considered my feelings. They weren't the ones trapped in this special hell. Although I knew the chemo was ravaging her body, I felt little compassion for her anger, no matter how justified she believed she was.

"And what nightmare is that?" I spat out viciously.

Her frail hand reached out for mine. I wanted to jerk it away, but knew better. I was experiencing my own emotional turbulence, and Raina felt the need to connect with me through this rage. "That he will fall in love with you, just to have you vanish from his life forever."

I closed my eyes and felt the air catch in my throat.

Julian was in love with me.

My head dropped as I held the sobs in, so as to not disturb any of the other patients distracted by our exchange. I couldn't stop myself from falling against her hollow chest and weeping uncontrollably.

Her delicate hand gently stroked the back of my head as she soothed my heartache with her sweet voice. "Do you love my son?" she asked quietly.

I nodded my head slowly.

Raina laughed and continued to comfort me. "Then you need to go to him, and make that stubborn child of mine realize that he's about to screw up the greatest thing that's ever happened to him. Okay?"

Although my chin quivered uncontrollably, I promised to go to him later in the day, but explained that I was to stay with her for the remainder of her treatment. My eyes followed the PICC line into her port that administered the medication, and I watched the slow drips from the IV bag slide down. I knew the next day her bones would feel like they were on fire, and she would vomit repeatedly. She had lost a great deal of weight and, although the chemo was giving her a few more days here on earth, her quality of life was rapidly declining.

"I am so sorry, Raina. I know I am a selfish, petulant brat. It's hard for me to sit here watching everyone go through this and feel bad about my situation. I hope you can forgive me."

I sighed heavily and leaned my head into her lap.

Raina laughed lightly and coughed a few times after. "Child, I know what it's like to feel like a stranger in your own body. To not have any control, or answers as to why things are so. How painful it is to move through the day to day, and continuously give yourself a reason to fight, when all you want to do is just go to sleep and have it all be over and done with. Tell me why am I sitting here voluntarily having my body poisoned to fight this demon, when I know ultimately I am going to lose? Why do any of us here keep fighting?"

I looked around and all eyes were upon us. The room had fallen silent, and not one person dared to respond. Raina's hand reached out for my cheek and was quickly soaked with tears. I didn't have to ask why. I knew.

"For love," I choked out.

Raina smiled as her own tears fell. "Yes, Stella, we fight for love, which you must do as well. Although our battles are different, we are still fighting the same war. Rich or poor, black or white, sick or healthy, there is only one force on earth that is strong enough to conquer the darkness; a force we crave like a drug and is just as vital as the air we breathe. We all need and want love. There are far worse things than death. To not know love is one of them."

I smiled and looked around at the others, who too had either thin streams of tears running down their faces or bright smiles. It was true. For all that we go through in life, what drives us forward can be summed up in one word—love. Granted it can be focused on sex, power, or money, but still. It is the love of it. It is the hope that the object of our affections will somehow fill the hole in our hearts and make us complete. Some of us find out all too late that anything less than authentic love is a poor substitute for the real thing, and only when we are about to take our last breaths can we see the consequences of a life lived selfishly.

I wanted to give Raina a fraction of the beautiful gift she had just given me. How quickly her words soothed my inner beast. Her strength was awe inspiring and her resilience motivating. There was nothing I could give this woman, other than my time and love, in return. As I reflected repeatedly on her words, I noticed a few individuals moving in time with the melody that was gently piped in over the speakers. I knew this song somehow. I started to hum softly, and I could feel it grow louder as each measure flowed through my veins. This was my therapy. I loved music. Something about it pushed through my pain and ignited my soul. Tapping my hand against my knees, I started to find a rhythm with various slaps and mumbled notes in my throat. I closed my eyes, parted my lips, and felt the words rush out of my lungs and into the silence.

When my eyes opened, Raina's hand began to slip from mine as she smiled and succumbed to sleep. I covered her with the extra blanket she had brought, and left for the remainder of the treatment.

I closed the door softly behind me, and one of the nurses gently touched my arm. "Pardon me. You are Stella Brady, right?"

I grew stiff and looked around cautiously. "Yes. Can I help you?"

The woman looked flustered and embarrassed. She reached into her pocket, pulled out a small notepad, and handed it to me. "I know you are here with someone, and I hate to ask, it's just, I can't believe you are here right now, and you just sang to our patients. It means so much, you have no idea how incredible this is."

I took the notepad and shook my head. "I didn't mean to bother anyone. Raina Moreau is a good friend of mine. I am here to support her, that's all," I said quietly.

"Bother? Are you serious? People are going to be talking about this for a long time to come. The one and only Stella Brady was at our hospital! This is a big deal, you don't have to be so shy about it. Oh, oh, oh . . . I was going to ask if you could please sign that for me."

I held the pen and paper in my hand apprehensively, before scribbling my name and handing it back. No one had asked me to sign an autograph yet. Then again, no one has had a chance to ask me. I could see she wanted to start asking questions, but I excused myself before she had the chance. Rushing out the automatic doors, I looked around and sought out a quiet bench against the trees. While breathing in and out deeply, I finally lifted my head and looked around. Countless people were walking the campus, enjoying the sunshine and beautiful day.

Raina was unable to sit out here, as the chemotherapy made her skin so sensitive she would burn within minutes. The birds sang happily as a gentle breeze swept across my skin. The smell of antiseptics was replaced by the sweet aroma of cedar from the freshly-laid mulch chips at my feet. Various colorful annuals were planted in beautiful displays, and families and friends visited among the professional colleagues enjoying lunch.

This was my life. Not the one I had lost, and not the one I felt I deserved. This moment was all I was guaranteed, and I was letting it slip away. An urgency rattled my nerves, but I forced myself to be still, breathe in the warm summer air, and listen as the children who ran past me on the sidewalk laughed. I looked up into the periwinkle sky and gazed at the billowing nimbus clouds floating across, threatening rain with traces of deep gray at the edges. Life was all abuzz around me, but I had been too caught up in the noise that resided solely between my two ears. For an hour I watched as others went about their day, and absorbed the beauty of a North Carolina summer. The humidity had not yet set in, and the days were as close to perfect as they'd ever been.

I was within view of the front door, and watched as my mother pulled into a parking spot. Before she could reach the entrance, I called out and beckoned her over to me. She appeared heavy footed, but I was not moved. She had every reason to be pissed off at me, and I imagined she would feel quite smug with my remorse.

A few paces away from the bench, she saw my face and slowed down. "Stella, are you okay?"

I shook my head and tried to hold back the tears, but I failed miserably and ran into her arms. "Mama, I am so sorry," I wailed.

She held me tight and moved from side to side. "Oh, Stella bug. I am sorry I snapped at you. I shouldn't have been so cross, it's just that I feel like everything is falling apart."

I smiled weakly and pulled her closer. "It is, mama, but this is how it's meant to be right now. Sometimes things have to fall apart so God can put them back the way he wants them. It won't always be this way."

Just as I'd cried against Raina's chest, I held my mother against mine. The woman who could move mountains, suddenly felt small in my arms. An urge to protect her and shelter her from any harm flooded my soul. This was love.

For nearly fifteen minutes, she wailed in my embrace. Her tears soaked my shirt, leaving a massive wet stain. But I didn't care, they were healing. We walked hand in hand to the oncology department and waited for Raina to be discharged. While I stood in the lobby, my mother went to retrieve the car. I pushed the umbrella-covered wheelchair to the curb, and helped my mother lift Raina into the seat. As we began the short trip back to Mooresville, my mother continued to smile into the rearview mirror at her best friend. They woke up expecting the worst, and could rest knowing that it would somehow work itself out.

I asked my mother to take me to the vineyard after we dropped Raina off at her house and got her situated. I had never been there, but I knew that's where Julian would be.

The sun would be setting shortly, and a stunning gold aura was cast onto the trees, reflecting from the shiny leaves. My mother was quiet as we moved out of town and in the direction of the vineyard was located.

After pulling to a stop, my mother kissed my cheek and held the side of my face for a moment. "Stella, remember he feels just as lost as you do. Show him he is not alone. He needs you more than you realize."

"What about Kai, mama? He cares about me too."

Her eyes closed and her lips tightened.

"I will not argue that Kai is a not a good man, and in a different world he may have been the one. But he's not. This is where you belong, and Julian is the reason I never told you. I wasn't trying to keep you from the truth. I simply wanted you to be able to discover it in your own time. Everything happens for a reason Stella, and this is no accident."

I nodded my head and opened the door of the truck. As far as the eye could see, grape trellises lined the horizon. I crossed the street and headed into the massive stone building. Inside there was a gift shop and restaurant. I inquired if anyone knew where I could find Julian, and a young man was dispatched with a small gator type of vehicle to escort me into the field. I hopped in nervously, and the kid sped off toward the lake. I held the side railings as we bumped along, but he was not shaken. The cool air brushed my face, and the sweet scent of grape vines and cultured soil permeated my nostrils. Feeling my body jerk, I closed my eyes and waited for it to pass.

Chapter 17

~ Strange Dreams ~

I awoke with a start, but was no longer in the gator where I had apparently lost consciousness. I was in a big bed, wearing a large T-shirt that smelled freshly laundered compared to the hint of musk emanating from the pillowcase. The moon illuminated the massive room, yet I was unsure where I was, and desperately needed to relieve myself. A door was left slightly ajar, and a night light beyond showed that it opened to a luxuriously appointed bathroom. My jaw dropped at the rustic opulence, reminiscent of something Tuscan. Marble lined the floors, while the walls and counters had intricately-painted tiles as accents. Plush towels rested in various places, with woven containers holding soaps, wash clothes, and extra toilet paper.

In the corner was a large walk-in shower without a door, and against the window was a massive tiled garden tub, sunken into the ground and large enough for several bodies. Unsure of how long I had slept and whose bed I had crawled out of, I took a peek into the medicine cabinet, hoping for a clue before allowing myself to panic. A few red bottles sat neatly at the top, with the basic staples indicating a woman did not share this space. I took one down and peered at the label, then smiled slightly before scrunching my brow. I was with Julian, but where?

I set the bottle back, tip toed into the bedroom, and carefully lifted back the sheets. I slid my arm over to feel for his body, and continued to reach until I realized I was alone. My mind had fully awakened, and began to race with unanswered questions. Unable to return to sleep, the overwhelming urge to soak away my concerns won out, and I began to pour hot water into the tub while exploring the rest of the room. A built-in shelf held several bottles of scented bath oils, beads, and salts. I picked them up, and they each smelled very expensive, which made me wonder who they belonged to, because men typically did not own such things. A layer of dust gently rested on the top, indicating they had never been used and were most likely decoration, which set my mind at ease.

I poured a concoction of vanilla, sandalwood, and English rose into the steaming water, then stripped down bare. The steps leading into the water felt pretentious, but I knew better than to pass up such an opportunity. It felt like forever before the water covered the edge of my breasts, but the temperature never once grew tepid.

While sinking down low, I glanced at the slightly-cracked door and realized someone was watching me. "You can come in, you know," I said, unafraid.

Slowly, the door opened, and a worn Julian shuffled in with wild hair and basketball shorts. He sat in the chair next to the bathtub, and rubbed his eyes. I had woken him, unaware of what time it really was. "I assume you are okay now?" he asked sleepily.

I tilted my head to meet his gaze. "I am okay now, though I have no clue what happened. One moment I was in the cart to find you, the next thing I knew I was waking up in a bed that's not mine. I am convinced this is all some strange dream, and I am just working my way though it until it is over."

Julian began to rouse and pulled off his white socks. "This is just a dream to you? You don't think any of this is real?"

I gently brushed my palms against the bubbles that rested across the surface of the water. "I am not sure what this is," I replied.

Julian scooted out of the chair and sat on the floor next to me, dipping his hand in the water and moving it back and forth. "What do you want this to be?" he asked.

Seeing him evoked a rush of blood through my body, and awakened an appetite that was reserved for him alone. The primal urges surfaced and, although I was furious for how easily I was dismissed, I now knew better. He was as helpless as I was in our ability to contain feelings for one another.

"I want you to get in here with me and help me figure it out."

Julian's eyes darkened, but he did not hesitate. He slid off his shorts, walked slowly down the steps, and reached out for me to stand. Accepting his outstretched grasp, I slid my body against his and trembled with anticipation.

Using his index finger, Julian lifted my chin to meet his unwavering stare. "Do you have any clue how crazy you make me?"

I nodded my head and felt myself grow weak. Julian's

mouth careened wildly into mine, stealing the breath from my lungs, and I was helpless to resist. He broke the kiss with haste, turned my body around, and instructed me to hold the edge of the bathtub. His large fingers splayed across my hips and jerked me backward into the desired position. With me bent at the waist, he explored the skin along my spine with his hands, then ran them down my thighs, eliciting a shiver. The oils allowed him to glide across my skin without resistance, which he used to his advantage. Slick fingers danced teasingly between the back of my thighs, before light slaps were administered onto the damp skin. I braced myself on my elbows and pushed back against him, hungry for more.

"Please," I said, moaning.

"Please what?" he asked.

"More. You," I mumbled.

Julian's hand pressed hard into my lower back before sliding around to my abdomen drawing me closer to him. I could feel his arousal press against me, waiting for the right moment. He dipped his mouth into the crook of my neck, and taunted me with gentle bites and roaming hands. "I'm sorry about the boat, Stella. I'm scared. I can't lose you. Not again. I don't know what I would do if . . ."

I spun around quickly and grabbed Julian's neck, pulling him closer. Holding the sides of his face, I made my plea. "Then don't let me go, Julian. Fight for me. Don't just let me slip through your fingers because you are afraid. I cried out another man's name because you weren't there to save me. I sought him out because you pushed me away. I won't stay here if you don't want me, but you have to tell me that you need me, that I still have a place in your heart."

Julian's lip quivered slightly as he nodded his head, but he still did not speak. It was all the affirmation I needed.

"Then I am yours," I said. I didn't care about Kai in this moment. One night with a stranger could not possibly negate years of proven devotion. As much as I hated to admit it, my mother was right.

His teeth softly pulled at my bottom lip as his hands slid behind my thighs. He then lifted me out of the water, before walking through the hall and back onto the bed.

As his body sank deliciously into mine, I smiled and looked around. "Where are we?" I laughed.

Julian kissed my neck and pressed harder with his hips, causing me to cry out. "We are in my apartment. I live here at the vineyard."

I wanted to ask more questions, but he silenced me with first his finger, and then his agile tongue.

"Soon enough, Stella. I will tell you anything you want to know."

I giggled and leaned up to bite his chin. "It doesn't matter, because you will keep me safe and that's all I need to know."

Chapter 18

~ Puzzles ~

The sounds of the field equipment woke me up before the sun pouring through the windows did. The workers must have arrived to start tending to the property as Julian slept securely next to me. Something told me he didn't sleep much, so I gently slipped out of the bed and peeked out onto the vineyard. A low fog snaked along the trellis leading up to the stone building. Although I was excited about getting to explore again, I decided to crawl back into bed and steal a few more uninterrupted moments of privacy. On my way back to the bed, I noticed the same thin layer of dust covered nearly every surface, indicating he was absent from here quite often. For some reason, I always assumed he lived with Raina, so this left me a bit perplexed.

However, watching Julian sleep overrode any curiosities of the moment. Doubt sat heavily in my stomach, hoping he wouldn't regret another night of being with me and throwing us back into the same vicious cycle. Covered only by a sheet, I let out a short giggle at the tented appearance beneath his navel. The more I looked, the more I was unable to resist running my fingers over the soft cotton. Julian's cock twitched beneath the soft grazing, which fueled my interest even more.

A smiled pulled at the corner of his lips before his eyes cracked slightly. "Having fun?" he asked with grit in his voice.

"I am about to, if that's okay with you. Not really sure what I am doing, but I figure I will learn as I go. I know I am not supposed to use teeth, right?"

Julian's eyes opened a bit more before giving another smirk. "No teeth, please. That would be appreciated. As for technique, just follow your instincts. I won't complain."

Licking my lips and raising my brows, I pulled the sheet back and watched him spring forward. I straddled his knees, leaned on one elbow, and gently began to discover what brought Julian pleasure. Every time I looked into his eyes, he grew harder in my hand. The small droplets formed at the head and tasted unlike anything I knew. As my tongue began small strokes along the base, Julian stopped me with a laugh before flipping me onto my back.

"Okay, Stella. It's been fifteen minutes, and I can only hold out for so long. I'm sorry, I need to come or I will lose it."

"Was it okay?" I asked with concern.

Slowly, Julian teased my center, before filling me completely. Clutching his shoulders, I pulled him close.

He turned his lips into my ear and paused. "It was perfect."

"Liar," I said, mocking him.

"Listen, the day a man claims anything less with morning head is the day he stops getting it."

My brow furrowed and I looked away. "I want you to enjoy it. I know I don't remember how to do it, and I just don't want you disappointed."

Julian pulled my chin back toward him and fixed on my gaze. "Stella, there is nothing you could do to disappoint me. Even fully clothed and covered in flour, you are the sexiest thing on earth. This is all the proverbial frosting on the cake."

"Mmmm frosting. I am starving!" I said.

With a shimmy of his hips, Julian brought me back to more pressing matters. "Oh, I'm sorry. We need to get you taken care of first."

I couldn't help but laugh loudly, before locking my ankle across his hip and rolling over. Sitting up, I winced slightly from the change of position and placed my hands on his chest for leverage. "Put your hands on my hips."

Julian did as I said and waited for further directions.

"Show me how you want me to move."

His hands began to gently press back and forth. I followed his lead, and watched his teeth clench each time I pressed down. I started moving faster, and his fingers dug into the soft flesh and pulled roughly.

"Fuck, Stella," he growled.

A moment later, I felt him swell and pull my hips down hard, holding them still as his body jerked beneath me. Panting hard, I collapsed from the unexpected workout, and felt my skin warm against his slick chest.

"Better?" I asked.

"Mmmmhmmm. Much. Thank you."

Kissing his collar bone, I replied, "You're welcome."

I lounged as long as he allowed me to in the embrace. A short span of time passed before he reminded me he had to get up. The only clothes I had were from the day before, and they would have to do.

"Do you want to see the vineyard?" he asked.

My enthusiasm was tangible. "Absolutely," I shrieked.

We walked down the stone stairwell and through the private access door. The morning air was thick and humid. Sunlight glistened from the large green leaves and small clusters of juicy grapes. I closed my eyes and absorbed the way the vines felt in my hands. The fruit was nearly ready, and would still be sweet. I plucked a grape, popped it into my mouth, and smiled.

"Muscadine are my favorite. It's a good thing they do well down here. Another week and you will be ready to press."

Julian stilled and looked at me cautiously. "How do you know that?"

I shrugged my shoulders and pinched a few clusters off with my fingernails. "I just do."

We continued to walk the path that lead to the top of a hill. A steep grade continued until we were able to look out over the entire vineyard and onto to the lake. A small wooden bench rested in a clearing, perfect for watching sunsets. The property was gorgeous, and brought forth a feeling of comfort.

"I know this place," I said.

Julian smiled and reached out for my hand, squeezing

slightly. "You loved being here and spending time working in the field. You said that vines were full of history, and so reminiscent of humanity, since they both had to be treated in a similar fashion, loved carefully, and tended to constantly for the best harvest. Such a hearty but delicate fruit."

I leaned my head against his shoulder and never wanted to leave. "You should let me buy it, Julian. I have the money, and that way you know it will always be taken care of when you leave."

His body stiffened at the request. "I'm sorry, Stella, but it's too late. Your mom actually introduced them to the buyers Darrick and Victor were the best candidates. They have been customers of ours for several years, and own a wine bar in Cincinnati. Victor travels a lot for his job, and Darrick has been waiting for the right opportunity to focus on crafting his own blends. I guess Victor used to work with Sandy at a hospital in Columbus. I am not sure if you ever met him."

I nodded my head. "They sound great. You're right, I don't know the first thing about running this place. It would be silly of me to buy it. Just because I can remember a grape, doesn't mean I should own a vineyard. It was just a thought."

Julian kissed the top of my head before standing. "I think you will feel better after you meet them. We're all going out for dinner when they arrive. I am surprised your mom didn't say anything to you."

"Eh, there's a lot she doesn't tell me. I am not surprised in the least, but she always has her reasons."

Exhaling deeply, I took one last look at the lake. "She's made an extra effort to avoid the topic of all things Julian for the past few weeks."

Julian stopped and looked at me sadly. "I'm so sorry, Stella. I don't know how to make it up to you. That was a really shitty thing to do."

I reached my arms around his waist and pulled him close. "Don't do it again, or I am going to kick your ass. Deal?"

He pressed his mouth against my neck, and the hot breath warmed my skin.

"Deal."

Chapter 19

~ Surprise ~

The days and nights passed quickly, as they filled with new memories. Julian and I were inseparable once again, which brought peace to our families. I accompanied Raina to her chemotherapy treatments, and worked in the field on other days. The sale would not be complete until the fall. Due to complications with the equipment, Julian decided to wait until after the harvest to proceed. I was still able to meet Darrick and Victor, and agreed they would be fantastic owners of the Moreau Vineyard. My mother enjoyed the company of an old friend, and Julian loved being able to talk about his work in New York. Darrick and I escaped to the lake and took a canoe onto the calm water.

"I think you will really like it here. It's a very special town. Everyone is really nice and, of course, the vineyard is thriving. I can help you if you ever need it after Julian leaves."

Darrick looked at me confused. "Aren't you two

together? Why would you be staying?" he asked curiously.

I felt the tears start to creep up and refused to let them fall in front of a stranger, no matter how quickly I was growing fond of him.

"Julian plans to go to New York. I am not ready to leave Mooresville. Not very many people know, but I have amnesia. I get overwhelmed really easy. New York would put me into a tailspin. And besides, Julian has spent the last two years caring for his mom, and he doesn't need to take me on. We want to be together, but he deserves a life of his own. I will be okay here. I plan on going back to school, anyway."

Darrick did not look convinced, but smiled and continued to paddle around the cove. As we tied to the dock, he stood first and helped me out. "You know, real love doesn't happen easily. There are always challenges, and they are meant to test you for the harder stuff down the road. You need to know your partner will be there with you through any storm. If you and he are meant to be, it will happen. Don't give up so easily."

I nodded and swiped away the rogue tear.

Darrick pulled me into a hug and laughed. "And honey, I see how he looks at you. I don't see him being away very long. I know that look. That man is in love with you."

I smiled and thanked him. "I hope you know that you aren't going to get rid of me either. I think we will both need the company," I said with a lighter heart.

"Anytime, darling," he replied.

As we made our way back up to the house, my mother had the citronella torches burning on the patio and a full spread with several bottles of wine on the table. Darrick handed me a glass, and I held it tentatively. Looking at Julian, I was unsure if I should drink. I hadn't since my accident, and wasn't sure how I would react.

"A little will be fine, Stella," he said reassuringly.

I tilted the glass to my lips, and the sweet wine covered my mouth in the most delicious flavor. I swirled it over my tongue, feeling a slight tingle, and then sharp notes of berry. I beamed at another part of my memory awakening.

"It's amazing. I will have to watch myself, this is way too easy to drink." I laughed.

The others toasted their glasses, and began conversing about the wine bar in Ohio and how it had expanded. Across the table, I caught Julian stealing glances of me slowly becoming drunk. I would look over at Darrick, who would give me a sly wink. I wanted more than anything to believe I was enough for Julian. Even though I told him to fight for me, I never pushed for him to stay. I refused to be selfish and ask him to give up more of his life, no matter how badly I wanted him in mine.

Late evening fell upon us, and I yawned sleepily. Taking note, the others excused themselves to bed and thanked my mother for the lovely evening. Julian went to get his keys, and I grabbed them from his hands.

"Um, no. You are not driving. You can stay here with me," I demanded.

He looked at my mother, who just smiled lazily. I had never seen her so carefree. I took a mental note to get her drunk more often.

"Excuse us," Julian said with a grin, as I dragged him into the house.

As soon as I closed the door to my room, my mouth crushed into his. He fell loudly back on the bed and chuckled hysterically. Ignoring his tickles, my hands successfully removed his shirt, although I felt as if I were fighting an octopus.

"Wow, you are feisty tonight, Stella. I like it." Julian's words slurred a little which I found endearing.

"You are drunk, and I plan on taking advantage of it. But I know I could if you were sober too, I just want to see what you will do."

Suddenly, he was no longer pliable to my tactics. With one swift motion, his arm wrapped my waist and flipped me onto my back.

"You want to see what I will do?" he challenged. His kisses were laced with tart fruit, making me even more delirious and provoking my ornery mood.

"Do your worst," I said daringly.

With a mischievous smile, he lifted his hips to remove his belt. He wagged his brows then gently pulled my arms through the iron spindles of the headboard and tied the belt loosely. I could easily slip out, but I knew he was going for effect.

"You like me helpless, do you?" I teased.

"I like you holding still while I drive you crazy."

I closed my eyes and melted beneath each sweltering pass of Julian's tongue. The wine had made me bold and I directed each move. "You said I was sweeter than any grape, and made you drunker than any wine, so prove it."

A dangerous grin curled at his lips as he slowly made his way down my abdomen. Jerking my knees apart, there was nothing gentle in his approach. Up until this point I felt as though he had been lenient with me, but craved something darker. Time had given him the ability to hone his desires and my little bouts of taunting let him know I was not shy. Two fingers plunged deeply and began to aggressively twist as his mouth ravaged my core. I was trying my best to stay quiet, but I was failing miserably, and mentally prepared for the morning confrontations. Before I could build up my mind, Julian unwound my body and dissolved all reason.

Unleashing my need was only the beginning of sating his. Keeping me bound, he flipped me onto my stomach to muffle the noises he was drawing from my body. I gripped the iron spindles until my fingers tightened with pain. My body stopped trying to resist and fell slack beneath him. Wrapping his arm beneath my chest, he pulled me close and whispered naughty things in between sharp bites and feather light kisses. He held nothing back as he claimed every inch of me as his own. With one final grunt, I was pinned in place to the mattress and only an explicit word to describe his height of his pleasure. "Fuck"

The next morning, Julian was gone from my bed, leaving only a curve of sheets and blankets where his body rested. I rubbed my wrists and smirked at the light red lines cutting into the skin. My head was pounding, and I desperately needed to brush my teeth. The clock said it was still early, but I could hear the clinking of pots and pans in the kitchen. I stumbled down the hallway and into the aroma of bacon and eggs sizzling in the iron skillets. All eyes fell on me with a knowing grin. Julian was at the helm, playing chef, and looking no worse for the wear. Leaning over to give me a light kiss, he held a smug look of satisfaction.

"Morning, sunshine."

I shook my head and shuffled to the coffee maker, stealing a piece of bacon from the plate on the way. He went to slap my hand away playfully, and I growled in return.

"Someone has her first hangover," my mother chimed in playfully.

I turned and put my hand up in the air. "You can all go to hell today."

The room busted out with laughter as I tried to find the bottle of aspirin in the cupboard.

My mother reached over me and pulled down the bottle with a knowing glance. "I told Julian if he broke your bed he was responsible for buying new one."

I looked over, but he refused to turn around, soliciting more laughter.

I cringed while bracing against the counter. "Can we please not talk about this?" I begged.

Sliding her arm around my waist, my mother kissed my cheek. "Were just playing, Stella."

I gave a sour look, made my way over to the table, and sat next to Darrick. He smiled brightly, and patted my leg.

A small grin pulled at my lips as I tilted the mug and took a small sip. "Okay so what's on the agenda today?" I was changing the conversation.

Julian set down the remaining eggs and grabbed a plate. "Well, Darrick and Victor need to go to the airport, so I thought you and I could take them and make a day of it. But first I have a surprise."

My ears perked up. "Surprise?"

Julian seemed enthralled by the secret he had planned.

"Yes, we must hurry, it might take a little bit, and they can't be late. We will come back here and pick them up, so go get dressed."

I bolted from my seat and pulled on a simple sundress and flip flops. Julian was at the door waiting for me, and we hurried to the truck. The summer sun was quickly making the day hot and sticky. We cranked up the air conditioner, but did not travel far before we pulled up in front of a small salon on the main street. All of the businesses were closed, being a Sunday, but a woman was waiting inside for us. She gave Julian a warm hug and turned to me with an extended hand.

"It's nice to finally meet you, Stella. My name is Liz. You must be very important to have someone like Julian seek out my services."

I skeptically eyed the gorgeous platinum blonde Asian woman who appeared so confident. She was definitely not someone Julian had mentioned before.

"And what exactly is it that you do?"

She smiled, while turning toward Julian and waiting for him to explain.

"Stella, you are afraid to leave because everyone recognizes you. Liz is here to change that. I asked her to come in especially for this. We were neighbors in New York. She is one of the most sought after makeup artists in the movie industry. She can teach you how to disguise yourself so you can go out in public without having to worry about privacy. You can be yourself."

"By being someone else?" I laughed.

Liz and Julian looked at me empathetically. Knowing how hard it had been, the gesture was incredibly sweet. I let out an exasperated breath and waited for direction. She led me to a chair in front of a mirror and, with her gentle hands on my shoulders, our eyes met in the reflection.

"Are you ready?" she asked with the most incandescent smile.

I nodded, then looked back at Julian and mouthed *"thank you."*

Silently, he replied, *"you're welcome,"* before taking a seat in the waiting area. In two long hours, I no longer recognized the person looking back at me. Even though I was unsure how I felt about the transformation, I trusted that no one would know who I was, and that was exactly what I needed.

Chapter 20

~ Mirror, Mirror ~

"Are you okay over there?" Julian asked with a laugh.

"Uh, yeah. It's just really weird. It's almost like looking into another dimension. It's me, but it's not."

Julian reached over and rubbed my leg affectionately. "It might take a bit to get used to. Just try not to think about it so much."

I smiled and went back to appraising Liz's craftsmanship. I had to hand to her. I couldn't imagine how much it cost to have her flown in the way he did for a private job. I offered to pay him for it when we got back into the car, and the insulted stare he gave was enough to shut me up. Every inch of my skin was free from blemishes, and not one trace of the ink beneath it showed. She assured me that the makeup was waterproof, and would not budge until I took a special cleanser she provided and a loofah sponge to it. I worried about it rubbing off on my dress, but as she promised, it stayed put.

Julian was almost afraid to come near me when Liz spun the chair around to unveil my new look. In addition to the tattoo coverage, she lightened my hair and trimmed it into a more fitting style. She also waxed, plucked, painted, and sculpted the rest of me. The most frightening part was imagining this was how I might have looked if my life hadn't gone in such a different direction. It started to become hard to look in the mirror with the sad thought.

Sensing me withdraw, Julian squeezed my hand firmly while massaging the palm with his thumb. "Hey, don't go there. I am not doing this because I think there is something wrong with how you look now. No matter what you do, you will always be beautiful. But you are different. I know you are ready to leave Mooresville too and rediscover who you are, but it must be done carefully. Not just because of the brain injury, but who you are to the public. I can't always be there with you to protect you, and I have accepted that. But if I can give you anything, it's today. One day to feel just like everyone else."

I wanted to cry, but knew there was no way I could reset an eyelash by myself if the tears dissolved the glue. I giggled at the thought alone.

"What's so funny?" he asked with his own grin.

"Just that I want to be emotional right now, but my face might melt."

We both busted out hysterically, and I had to hold back the tears of laughter, as well as those of joy. I wasn't sure what all Julian had in store, but I knew it had to be amazing. I thanked Liz with a giant hug and she handed me a maintenance bag and her card. I stared in the passenger mirror the entire ride back, disbelieving what was reflected. When we pulled up the driveway, I saw my father had returned from the church and was sitting with

Darrick and Victor waiting for our return. The unanimous approval made me blush, until I saw concern wash over my father's face.

"What's wrong, daddy?"

Was he feeling what I was in the salon only moments earlier? That this was the daughter he should have had, and not the ink-covered hell raiser he was given instead?

The corners of his mouth twitched as he tried to think about the best way to convey his thoughts. He reached out to grab my wrist, and turned my arm in different directions, looking over the covering.

He shrugged his shoulders and pulled me into a hug. "You know, when I first saw all of those tattoos, I thought they were the ugliest things on earth, and I couldn't for the life of me figure out why such a pretty girl would desecrate her body that way. But then I had to stop and realize that it has no bearing on your soul. God allowed you to walk down the path that he did for a reason, and who am I to argue with His plans? I am actually quite fond of them now. You have always understood that your battles were spiritual. You are just an angel in disguise."

I snorted and squeezed him tighter. "Daddy, I am no angel. Not even close. But I guess every father thinks of their little girl like that."

Raising his brows he looked up at Julian and my mother who were side by side, leaning on each other affectionately. "That they do," he replied.

Knowing that the guys needed to catch their flights, I nodded to Julian that we had better get going. He went and helped them load their luggage into the truck as they said their goodbyes and thanked my mother for her hospitality. The ride to the airport was brief, but knowing that Julian had a decision to make gave an air of seriousness. I stayed quiet as they discussed the details of the vineyard, and I noticed Julian's arm was tense on my leg. Placing my hand over his, I squeezed reassuringly and offered comfort. He was preparing to let go of a vital piece of who he was. I could think of no better owners than Darrick and Victor, and the connection to my family made it easier to accept. Raina was at peace with whatever Julian decided, knowing that it wouldn't matter once she passed, as long as he was okay with it.

After seeing the two men off, I wanted to ask what was going through Julian's mind, but I didn't have to. I could feel it pouring out of him. Years of waiting had finally come to an end, and soon he would be free to return to the life he left behind.

"I have another surprise for you," Julian said while turning the key to the ignition.

While licking the sugar from the cotton candy off my fingers, my eyes widened. "I don't know how much more I can take. Today was amazing. Not one person realized who I was. I think I might try and learn how to do my makeup, so I can sneak off again and not let this just be a one-time deal."

He used his finger to trail down the bridge of my nose, pinched the tip, then chuckled.

"I think that's a great idea. Now that you know it works, you have another tool for coping. You could even get really dramatic and wear wigs of different colors. I went with my mom to a hairstylist that the oncologist recommended. They showed her several kinds that are made of real hair and everything. I may or may not have tried a few on. I have to admit, I make a stunning red head."

"I bet you did." I remarked sarcastically.

As the truck began to drive off, I flipped down the visor mirror and could see thin lines forming in the creases of my face where the humidity was starting to degrade the cosmetics. Black smudges from the eyeliner rested in the corner, and the blush was all but gone. My arms remained covered, but the lines of separation were becoming more defined where it blended in on my wrists. Today had been so much more than I could have ever hoped for. Hours were spent exploring downtown Charlotte and walking the picturesque lake at Freedom Park.

"Thank you again for the millionth time, Julian. For the first time, I feel like everything is going to be okay, and that I can make something of this life. Your patients will be really lucky to have you back."

He gave a sideways smile, and I could see the tinge of sadness in his eyes. Despite the conversation of fighting for one another, a part of us still struggled with how it could ever be possible. Julian was adamant about returning to the Navy, and I wasn't ready to leave Mooresville and my family. A life in the military and away from them meant total dependence on Julian, and it was a burden I refused to impose on myself. Rather than arguing about the future, we made a silent agreement to focus on the present. With the sale of the vineyard pending, every moment seemed precious.

Upholding the agreement, Julian's hands reached for mine and he mindlessly rubbed deep circles into my palm.

"So how long have you been planning all of this?" I

asked.

He sat in thought and returned a tentative smile. "Not long after you arrived. When I heard you'd shaved your head, I knew immediately that you were suffering from body dysmorphic disorder. Sandy told me you said you felt like a monster because of all the tattoos. You did the only thing you felt like you could control. I wanted you to know that wasn't true. I just waited until you were comfortable in your skin again before suggesting it, and it seemed like the perfect time for it to be a surprise. I wanted it to be a positive experience. Not just another burden."

My heart continued to swell with a reverent joy at how much Julian cared. Before I had even laid eyes on him, he was already laying in motion the necessary means for my recovery. Grinning broadly, I leaned my head on his shoulder, after placing a lingering kiss and thanking him.

"I would do anything for you, Stella. I mean that."

I let the words sink in, and I knew they were true. He would do everything but stay. Continuing to banish the negative thoughts from my mind, I squeezed his bicep and enjoyed the ride. A short while later, we approached the entrance of a large park and waited patiently as cars filed in a long line. The sun was starting to set, and crowds of people carried lawn chairs and blankets with coolers. After finding a place to park, Julian lifted a rubber tote out of the truck bed and removed a soft cooler and duffle bag. A set of chairs was hidden under the tarp, wrapped to look as though it was some type of equipment.

"Wow, you weren't kidding when you said you had another surprise, were you?"

Giving me a wink, he handed me the chairs and locked

the truck. "I've always wanted to come here for this. I hope you enjoy it as much as I think you will."

Curiously, I scanned the lot and asked where we were.

"It's the Charlotte Symphony Summer Pops. They hold it here at South Park every year. It's right on the lake and, as you can see, draws a lot of people. I want to make sure we get a good seat, so we better hurry."

We walked swiftly to the entrance, and Julian handed the gate agent tickets. A crowd was moving swiftly down the paved path toward the outstretched covered stage. Securing a spot in the center of the field near the front, I was able to see every chair that was waiting for a member to arrive. Music and announcements piped over the loudspeakers, as more people filed in. Chatter filled the air all around us, anticipating the performance and lending an excitement to the atmosphere.

I removed the chairs from the fabric sleeves and propped them open, as Julian spread a blanket on the ground. I removed my shoes and felt the cool grass beneath my feet, then I made myself comfortable.

"I know we ate not too long ago, but are you hungry?"

I sat up and looked over the items Julian packed away for us, and realized he had a preference for certain foods.

"I will only eat if you don't act like an asshole in the morning," I mocked while cracking the lid on the chicken salad and taking a bite. Noticing his face become uneasy, I revealed the joke.

"You packed this the night we were on the boat."

He shook his head and continued to remove more items. "I like this food, and it keeps well in a cooler. I didn't notice. It's a coincidence."

Not wanting to set a sour mood, I sat on my knees and leaned in to give him a reassuring kiss. "I know, I was just trying to be funny. You know better now."

I lifted another forkful of food to my mouth, but it was knocked to the side when Julian tackled me to the ground and pinned me on my back. I squealed with laughter and wiggled out of his grip the best I could.

"I have been known on occasion to do very stupid things. Education is not an indication of intelligence. In matters of the heart, men are all imbeciles."

I nodded my head in agreement, and my body thrashed as fingers danced along every ticklish nerve in my body. Breathing hard, I wrestled between laughing and whining. With my arms pinned above my head, and my legs helplessly trapped under his, I knew we were creating a spectacle and cared nothing of it. Julian looked down at me with a satisfied smirk, and slowly leaned in to kiss me. It allowed the tension to leave my body, and I melted into the earth beneath him.

Effortlessly, Julian possessed the ability to take my breath away and leave me hungry for more. With every touch, I could physically feel the electric charge as my sensory neurons traveled with lightning speed to form a synaptic response. Dopamine flooded each crevice of my brain like a tidal wave. Surely this wasn't how love was, or so many people wouldn't fall out of it. How can it be possible for one human to evoke such a reaction in another?

Feeling dizzy with happiness, I smoothed my hair away from my face and blushed.

"I suppose things like that make up for our stupidity," he said.

"Hmmmmm?"

Julian's words came across garbled through the dream-like state. Roaring with laughter, he leaned in and bit my shoulder gently. "Nothing."

I smiled and curled into his arms as the orchestra members took their seats. Everyone began to clap as the conductor took his place on the podium. After a brief introduction, the wind ensemble began to warm up, as each section tested instruments in preparation for the show. The program was opened with "Summertime" from George Gershwin's opera "Porgy and Bess," and concluded with Vivaldi's "Summer Concerto."

My mind reeled at how beautiful the music was as it echoed over the lake. The sunset painted the sky in brilliant oranges, pinks, and blues, while the humidity kept the evening air comfortable. The fine hairs on my skin would raise with each Crescendo, and my eyes would close, feeling every note pulled from the bows of nearly twenty violins. Julian's fingers danced in time with the melody across my back, mimicking the conductors fluid hand gestures and burning his place into the memory.

The evening ended far too soon, then it was time to head back. While packing the chairs into the sleeves, the loudspeakers began to pick up where the orchestra had stopped. The first measure played, and the chair fell from my hands. Sinking to the ground slowly, I could no longer see the world around me, I was back in that place. I could hear Julian shout, but I was unable to move until the song had ended. Clawing through the darkness, I regained full consciousness and found my arms tightly gripped to Julian's tear-soaked chest.

I shook my head and started to back away, but he refused to let me move. Using his fingers to bring my chin up and my gaze to his, I could see fear racing through his eyes.

"Stella, what happened? I need you to tell me now," he demanded.

I closed my eyes again and breathed deeply. "Canon in d minor happened. That was the song I heard when I was coming out of the coma. I can remember not being able to move, and all I could think about was everything that I would never get to do in life. I thought I was going to be that way forever, and all I wanted to do was die. It was horrible." I started to sob and Julian pulled me close.

"It's okay, Stella. I'm here."

After a few more deep breaths, I was able to calm down enough to stand up. A small crowd of people stood around us, as Julian assured them I was alright. I was mortified at the outburst, but knew I had no control of how my brain chose to respond to things.

Walking toward the parking lot, I knew cracking a joke was the only way to ease the weight of the situation. "Remind me if I ever get married that I cannot walk down the aisle to that song. I might not make it to the altar."

Giving a weak laugh, Julian kissed the top of my head while squeezing my shoulder.

"Duly noted."

With the truck packed, Julian lifted my face to his once more and frowned. "Did you enjoy yourself otherwise tonight?" he asked.

I nodded my head and smiled. Using my fingers, I forced his lips into a floppy grin that he allowed to fall each time I moved them. "Yes, I did. It was incredible. Please don't be sad. I'm sorry that it happened. If that's the worst that happened to us today, then we are doing pretty well. The night is not over yet. We can still do something else to make sure it ends with a bang."

I reached my arms around his back and squeezed his rear, then he leaned down and growled in my ear before gently nibbling across my collar bone.

"What's with you and teeth today? I kind of like it . . . a lot," I said teasingly. I felt him smile against my neck, then he continued drag his teeth over the skin. I began to moan in delight, but I was interrupted by the continued vibration in Julian's pocket.

"Hon, you might want to get that. It's the fourth time in less than three minutes, I think it's important."

Reluctantly, Julian pulled the phone out and answered it. "Hello?" he asked with obvious annoyance at the disturbance. His face grew pale as squatted on the ground and listened.

"Yes, I'm here. Where? I will be there immediately."

I didn't have to ask what was wrong. Something had happened to Raina, and it wasn't good. Julian straightened out while the voice on the other line continued to speak. He motioned for me to get it the truck, so I strapped myself in and grabbed the door handle as he recklessly pulled out of the spot. Nervous that we were going to get into an accident, I asked Julian if he wanted me to drive. His arms were shaking as I reached out to touch him, and he flinched. He honked his horn at the cars impatiently, then he looked around and drove off of the street and into the immaculate lawns surrounding the park.

"Julian, what's wrong?" I shouted.

It wasn't until we were close to the highway that he

responded. Without taking his eyes off the road, he darted in and out of cars as fast as he could. I felt as though a police officer would get the call about us and begin searching for the truck any moment.

I closed my eyes and leaned against the headrest. I knew what this meant. Julian's nerves couldn't possibly take anymore, and this was the last thing he needed. I wanted to tell him it would be okay, but I couldn't. I didn't want to believe this was the end. Not today. Silently, I pleaded with God.

Just one day lord, please, just one day . . .

Chapter 21

~ Eleventh Hour ~

The truck could not get to the hospital fast enough. The call from the on-duty nurse had Julian cursing and banging the steering wheel repeatedly, while trying to shove the accelerator to the floor board. I tried to rub his back to soothe him, but there was no way to diffuse the adrenaline in his veins.

She was still breathing and her heart rate was stable, but there were too many unknowns. Raina suffered a heart attack and was holding on for dear life. The combination of toxic chemicals and voracious cancer had devoured her body to nearly a vapor. More often than not, she simply slept. The few hours she was conscious, were clouded by the morphine drip that never stopped. We knew this day was coming, and now the minutes were ticking by rapidly.

Julian whipped the truck cockeyed into a parking spot, and bolted to the front doors of the hospital without even turning off the ignition. I locked everything up, and trailed after him to the ninth floor where Raina was resting in the intensive care unit. The moment the elevator doors opened, I could hear shouting between the doctor and Julian, who was demanding to know his mother's status. I was thankful she was asleep and unable to witness her child in such distress. I jogged up to the door, and gently pushed Julian back to take a moment to breathe.

"Look at me. Dammit, look at me, Julian. Calm down, this isn't helping anything. Let the man speak," I said.

Wild eyed, he paused just long enough to anchor onto me and find his bearings. His palms squeezed my arms so tightly I knew they would bruise, but I gladly accepted whatever pain I could take away from him.

"I'm not ready yet. Not today. Not when everything has been so perfect. Just one day, Stella. Just one day I want to be fucking normal," he cried out.

Just then, a lightning bolt raced from my brain, down my spine, and electrified every nerve in my body. Julian was shaking too hard to notice the infliction, but unlike before, it didn't stop. The room began to spin, and I felt myself grow dizzy. I held onto Julian for stability, but he was too unbalanced himself, so we crashed into the wall and slid to the floor. Pain began to radiate through my skull, creating small tremors. I closed my eyes and held on to Julian as he wept. The anguish in his voice kept me from slipping away into a darkness that threatened to swallow me just an hour before.

The sharp aroma of disinfectants pierced my nostrils, and suddenly every noise was amplified. Every heart monitor, pulse oximeter, ventilator, and machines designed to sustain life echoed loudly. The stark chill of the hard cement floor penetrated my skin, and memories began to burst forth from the hidden chambers of my mind.

"This isn't happening," I murmured.

Lovingly, he began to stroke my hair and kiss my head, while rocking back and forth.

"I know, baby. I don't believe it either," he replied sadly.

He believed the torment I was expressing was over Raina and, in that moment, I refused to let him know any different. Quietly, I rested in his arms, swimming in the abyss of fear. There was no song to end and come back from. No definite moment the feeling would pass. Slowly, the woman I had become seeped through my veins and collided with memories of my present like an IV drip of narcotics. This reality was more strange and surreal than either one I had known before, and it took everything in me to process it. As Julian pulled me to my feet and into his arms, he held me briefly before wiping his eyes and stepping into Raina's room.

He walked around her bed and grazed his fingers along the tubes that were connected to multiple parts of her body. She was intubated, and unable to breathe on her own. After kissing her cheek, he fell to his knees and began to pray. How many times had this scenario played out before me? With a new set of eyes, I scanned the room and every detail scorched vividly with recognition. Feeling a sudden rush of nausea, I excused myself to the bathroom and gripped the cool porcelain as my stomach emptied itself violently. Over twenty excruciating minutes passed, and I could hear the doctors on the other side of the door speaking with Julian and discussing her prognosis.

"She will regain consciousness soon. We have

determined that, in addition to the myocardial infarction, she is suffering from coronary thrombosis. She may not survive any attempts to restore blood flow. We understand you do not want her to stay here, but please know that we are doing all that we can. Although we would prefer for her to remain in ICU for monitoring, a hospice nurse will be in shortly to discuss transporting her home. I am sorry; I wish I could do more."

I waited until the doctor left before cracking open the door and walking out slowly. Julian was sitting next to Raina, stroking her arm and talking to her softly. He looked up with red, swollen eyes, and silently pleaded for answers I did not possess. I gently crawled into his lap and cradled his head against my chest.

"You aren't alone, Julian. I'm here," I whispered, trying to offer any comfort I could.

"I don't know what I would do without you," he said in a raspy voice.

"You don't have to know," I replied.

As we held each other close, a light knock came at the door, and we both looked up. A middle-aged woman with short curly hair and a benevolent smile greeted us. *The hospice nurse.* She was wearing a khaki suit and hospital-issued name badge with smiley face stickers that were faded and wearing off. She reached out her hand to me, and then Julian, before looking at Raina sympathetically. I couldn't imagine having her job. As an intern I knew them well, because families almost always preferred their loved ones at home where they could be comfortable. Day in and day out, they wielded a brave smile and powered through the day helping to make a patients last wishes come to pass. I called them intercessors, because I felt it was the next step a person took before entering the gates of heaven, or in some cases, hell.

Feeling claustrophobic, I asked Julian if he was okay with me taking a short walk to get some air while he set everything up. When he nodded his head, I excused myself and headed for the elevator. The doors chimed on each floor, with people getting in and out. I leaned against the back rail, and looked down at the ground, trying to comprehend everything that was happening.

When the next rush of people came in, a familiar voice called out my name. "Stella? Stella Brady, is that really you?" the man asked.

I had paid no attention earlier, because the faces in white lab coats seemed to blend together. Once my eyes were able to focus, I could finally place him with the name. "Holy shit, is it really you Brandon?" I asked in disbelief.

He smiled as I reached out and ran my fingers across the stubble on his cheeks. Large brown eyes and a bright smile instantly propelled me into another place in time. Before I could protest, strong muscular arms pulled me close as his chest rattled in laughter.

"Holy shit is right. I thought I would never see you again. That is in real life, of course. More than a few of us have used you as our claim to fame. Wow, where have you been?" he asked joyfully, before his eyes stopped on the scar peeking down from my hairline. I nervously looked around and could tell we held a captive audience. Noticing my apprehension, he moved closer to block me against the wall until the elevator stopped at the next floor.

With an outstretched hand, he nodded his head to the door. "C'mon, Stella. Let's get you somewhere else."

With my hand in his, he could feel the sweat collecting

in my palm and the trembling in my body. My pulse was racing, and I felt myself growing nauseated again. I breathed in deeply to calm down, but needed to find a place to sit, or I risked passing out. Brandon stopped mid step and took a look at my face. He extended his hand, and used the pad of his thumb to pull under my eyes and examine the pupils.

"Stella. Something is wrong with you. Tell me how you're feeling."

I shook my head, and started to wobble in my footing.

"I'm going to be sick. Get me to a bathroom."

He rushed me into a room and opened the door. My knees hit the ground just before more bile came forward and burned my esophagus. Brandon shouted for help, and a team of nurses rushed into the room.

"Stella, I know you are freaking out right now. You are safe. I won't let anything happen to you. I need you to breathe. Do you have any drug allergies?" he asked calmly.

I shook my head and spit into the toilet bowl, anticipating another attack. He turned to a nurse and asked for a high dose of lorazepam, *stat.*

"You are going to be fine, I promise. Thank God I ran into you."

Taking a glance down, I could see his nametag near my waist as he crouched next to me on the ground.

Dr. Brandon Perry – Cardiology

"You fix hearts, Dr. Perry? What happened to obstetrics?" I laughed.

Feeling his hand press gently on my back, a rush of comfort came over me.

With humor in his voice he responded, "Well, I could only be around so many vaginas before I realized that job might scar me for life."

The nurses behind us snickered at the exchange, and a moment later one returned with the medicine and a plastic cup of water.

"Take this, Stella. We need to get you calmed down and find out what's going on. I am thrilled to see you, don't get me wrong, but I would prefer it wasn't as a patient."

Gratefully accepting the medicine, I allowed the water to drench my parched throat and reached out for a refill.

"Not too fast. You don't want to get sick again," Brandon said.

While sipping the water, I gave a middle finger and a wink.

"You're going to recover just fine, Brady. I have no doubt. Let's get you up and into the bed so I can determine whether or not you need to be admitted."

Suddenly, I remembered that Julian was upstairs with Raina, and most likely having a panic attack of his own.

"Julian, the ninth floor. I need to get back. He's waiting for me."

Brandon gently pushed my shoulders back and instructed me to wait a second. "Stella, you are showing signs of a generalized anxiety attack. Do you know what set it off?"

I looked around the room, and asked if we could be alone for a moment. He turned his head and silently dismissed the curious staff, then he turned back to me and waited for my response.

"Brandon, I was in a really bad accident. I am sure you know that. Up until about an hour ago, I have been suffering from retrograde amnesia. The only reason I know that is because my memories did not dissipate like I thought they would. It's like a puzzle that came together. I don't remember the coma, but I remember coming to, and for months I couldn't remember anything. You, any of it. Earlier tonight, I heard a song and it was like I was waking up again, and I couldn't move. When we got here, Julian said something, and it was like a light switch went on. Now, I don't know what to do, and . . ."

"Sssshhhhhhh . . . I told you. You are safe here. Oh, Stella. I don't even know where to begin. I think you need to be admitted for observ . . ."

"No!" I shouted. "I need to get back to Julian. He needs me. He can't know I have my memory back. Not today. Please, I am begging you. Just get me back to the ninth floor. Pretend you don't know me. I can't explain everything now. I will, though. I promise. Just not today."

Hot tears began to pour down my cheeks, and he could sense the desperation in my voice. My heart began to pound again, and I could feel the anxiety creeping up.

Brandon pulled the penlight from his corner pocket and asked me to hold still. "Stella, I really think you need to be seen. This isn't something I can just let go. As a doctor and a former colleague, but most of all, we were friends. You disappeared without a trace over a decade ago, and you just happen to reappear in the same elevator as me. Your mom . . ."

I shot out of the bed and was inches from his face, stopping him mid-sentence. "No one can know, especially my mother. If I let you do an exam, will you let me go? I promise to come back for more testing."

Reluctantly, he pulled out his stethoscope and instructed me to lay down. As the cool metal dial danced across my chest, I giggled. "Hey, you finally get to touch my boobs. There's a bright side to everything."

He looked at the ceiling and bit back a smile. "I'm really worried about you, Stella. More than that, I really missed you. You have no idea. We all did. And that prick Jefferson finally got what was coming to him."

My head snapped and my eyes zeroed in on his. I could feel my breathing increase, and I saw him grow concerned.

"You never knew, did you? He's in jail, Stella. He lost his license and was found guilty of malpractice. You vanished before the trial, but it was a really big deal. Because of you, they discovered he had been using students to perform delicate procedures and administer medications outside of protocol. Mr. Davies told the court what happened before you gave him the blood pressure medication. He said he saw you question the doctor about the dosage because of his systolic numbers, and Jefferson told you to do your job. It wasn't your fault."

Brandon's words fell into my heart like a meteor. Aside from the call about Julian that night, the near death of Mr. Davies was the catalyst for my tailspin into self-destruction. I was unable to forgive myself for letting something so deadly happen by my hand. I felt as though I had no right becoming a doctor, and subsequently let my life fall apart. That one moment led me to believe an imaginary shame that ran so deep, and I did everything I could to escape the pain. Half of my life had been spent hiding from a lie.

A buried wail thundered from my lungs and rattled my

soul. A stream of absolution flowed out of my heart and through my burning eyes. Brandon sat on the bed and pulled me into his arms, as I was finally granted reconciliation with the past. Was it possible that the almighty orchestrated this entire coincidence to bring me to this very juncture in time? There was no other explanation. The gravity of the situation was too much to comprehend, and I finally stopped trying. As the sobbing subsided, I could feel the sedative beginning to lull me into a tranquil state. With heavy eyelids, I mumbled out my request, "Take me to Julian, please. Room nine-fourteen."

Brandon released me to lie on the bed, then left the room, and returned with a wheel chair. He gently lifted my body, then set it down and I floated back up to where Julian and Raina were waiting. Julian raced straight over to me, frightened, and cradled my lethargic head.

"What the fuck? What happened? Not you too!" he shouted with terror in his eyes.

Before he was able to get too worked up, Brandon raised his hands and asked him to calm down. "Julian, she's going to be okay. I am Dr. Perry. I went to school with Stella at UNC, and recognized her in the elevator. As we were talking, people got curious and she had a panic attack. I gave her a sedative to calm her down. She's been really worried about you, and I promised I would bring her back as soon as I knew she was more settled. I told her she needs to come back and get a few tests, but I promise, she's fine. Just a little shaken. From what I can see, I understand why. Do you mind if I ask what's going on?"

After a few deep breaths and a shower of kisses, he started to relax. "Stella, I swear you are going to give me a heart attack."

Brandon laughed and flicked his name tag. "Good thing I was the one that brought her back then."

With a weak smile Julian shook his head. "Thank you for returning her to me. It's been a long day. My mom had a heart attack, and earlier tonight, Stella . . . it's just been a fucked up night. We're getting ready to take her home."

Brandon logged into the laptop and began to assess Raina's charts. A heavy weight fell over the room and he looked at me with a silent understanding.

"Mr. Moreau, I am really sorry. If there is anything I can do for you, please, don't hesitate to call." He reached into his pocket, pulled a card out, and handed it to Julian.

After shaking his hand, he walked back over to me and crouched to the ground so he could look into my eyes. "As for you, Brady, take it easy on this guy." He laughed.

Before leaving the room, he stopped and patted the doorway. "Moreau. Julian Moreau. That's you?" Brandon asked.

Julian stood up and replied, "Yes. Is there a reason you are asking?"

Brandon smiled broadly and looked at me before returning his attention to Julian. "I used to be very jealous of you. Stella would never shut up, and it was as though you walked on water. I would have to remind her to take off your dog tags before going into radiology. I told myself that one day I would be half as lucky as you to find a woman like her. It's a pleasure to finally meet you, soldier." He raised his hand in a salute, which Julian reciprocated.

Through my sideways view, I grinned at Julian as best

I could.

He fell onto his knees at my feet, rested his head on my lap, and closed his eyes. "Do you have any idea how freaked out I am right now? It's a damn good thing I love you, Stella Brady," he said quietly.

I reached my hand out to comfort him, but it flopped on his face, causing him to wince in pain.

Feeling myself falling asleep, I mumbled out as well as I could, "I lurveee youuu tooo."

Chapter 22

~ Finish Line ~

Raina's house continued to be a buzz of activity, as different medical companies were in and out exchanging tanks, delivering medications, and issuing paperwork. My father stepped in at the bakery, so Julian could be home with her. My mom took a leave of absence, and asked another physician to be on call. At Julian's request, she monitored Raina's care, lovingly ensuring that she was in the least amount of pain possible. When she was awake, she demanded we smile and share stories of happy times. I noticed her eyes sparkle the most when Julian and I were next to one other, giving each solace.

I had to force Julian to eat and sleep. When he did, it wasn't very much, and he wasn't able to unless I was there with him. When he would finally fall asleep, I'd slip away to visit Raina and monitor her vitals. Occasionally, she would wake and realize I was there, then hold my hand as she went back to sleep. I tried to withhold the tears from all of the time I missed being away, knowing it was gone forever.

A week had passed, and she was still hanging on. Her breath was labored, and her weight had plummeted. I half joked I could find her a marijuana brownie if it helped to give her a bit of an appetite, smiling at the thought of getting stoned with her. One afternoon, my mother and Julian were both out running errands, leaving me alone with the hospice staff. Raina was particularly alert, and ushered them out the door. I paid little attention to the emphasis she assured them with, and I told them I would call if something happened. Reluctantly they left, knowing it was necessary. I grabbed a cup of coffee, turned on the television, and flipped to her favorite soap opera. A few minutes into the show, she asked me to turn it off.

"Do you want to watch something else?" I asked.

She turned her head slowly toward me and took a deep breath. "No, I want to talk to you." Her voice was low and wheezy from the fluid building in her lungs. The oxygen tank ticked as air pumped through the small tubing, causing me to check the pressure levels.

"Sure, what's up?"

As my fingers untangled the pile of tubing next to the bed, she reached out and touched my arm. Looking at her face, I knew it was something serious.

"When do you intend on telling them you have your memory back?" she asked solemnly.

Frozen in place, I wasn't sure how to respond. I allowed the tubing to fall out of my hands and took a seat next to her. "How did you know?"

Tilting her head, she gave a knowing smile. "Very little escapes me. I know when you are out here, tinkering with the machines and talking to yourself. I know that you talk to me. I hear you praying, and crying. I am surprised no one has caught on yet."

I let out a deep breath and pulled my knees up to my chest. "I don't know. It's hard. I have all of these feelings, and no way of expressing them. I'm not ready to go back to the life I had. Not yet. The moment everyone knows, everything will change. There are so many things I have done wrong, and for what? Because of a misunderstanding? I know I can't pretend for very much longer, and you will probably disagree with my thinking, but I wasn't going to say anything until after the funeral. I know it will scare everyone."

Raina's hand squeezed mine lightly, and rather than giving me an argument on how I needed to tell them, she sought answers to the questions that rested in her heart.

"Stella, I need to know what happened to you to make you so afraid. I need to know the truth. What happened to you?"

Of all the memories I failed to recall, forgetting this one was impossible. It haunted my dreams and surfaced every time I felt I could open myself to someone. It was the cement in the stone walls built around my heart, and fueled the anger that drove me forward. The familiar rage boiled in my veins just thinking about the point I was crushed to pieces.

My jaw clenched, forcing the misery back. I wouldn't cry over this. I had shed enough tears to last a lifetime, over a moment so painful, and I had grown numb to the emotional debt. Getting lost in the anger, the coolness of Raina's hand, brought me back to the present.

"Stella please, you can tell me."

There wasn't a single part of me that wanted to revisit that dark place, because doing so meant ripping open a wound I had spent years trying to heal. As I closed my eyes and pondered her request, the dial on her grandfather clock shifted and it began to chime, a poignant reminder of what was taking place.

I felt as if I was standing in front of a giant door I had nailed shut, and her plea was a crowbar begging me to loosen the nails. With everything that had transpired in the past week, I knew there was no point in avoiding the inevitable, and it was time to face the monster within. Pushing past the pain and discomfort, I reached into the deepest part of my soul and submitted to fate. The first tear seared a trail down my face, with many more to follow. Feeling her grip tighten, I knew I wasn't alone. The words choked in my throat, and my tongue grew thick and heavy.

Exhaling a ragged breath, I began the tale of my descent. "I hadn't slept in two days. It was finals week, and the hospital was understaffed due to the physicians being away for the holidays. Dr. Jefferies had a few of us doing rounds with him and the interns. We were just supposed to be observing. I received a call from Heather McHenry telling me that Julian had come home and she'd seen him at the airport. But he wasn't alone. He was with a pretty girl. They were laughing, and she kept touching him, but he didn't push her away. Heather knew I was waiting for him to come home and wanted to find out what was going on, so she approached him and he seemed really nervous. He begged her not to tell me about her, saying it was important that she didn't say anything. But she knew I would be devastated, so she found a payphone in the terminal and called me right away. I was in shock; I didn't know what to think.

I couldn't believe Julian would ever hurt me like that, but she saw it with her own eyes. I was so angry that when

Jefferies gave me the orders, I knew it was too much, and I questioned him, but I did it anyway. I almost killed Mr. Davies. He didn't deserve that. Jefferies threatened me, saying that if I said a word, I would never graduate. But I didn't care. How could I knowingly practice medicine knowing I could be so reckless?"

I wiped the tears away from my eyes, and could see Raina's face so full of heartache and anguish. Her arm trembled as it held mine firmly, refusing to let go when I needed her so desperately. She allowed me to cry for a few moments longer, then she took a deep breath and looked at the clock.

"Stella, I need you to go into my bedroom and open my top drawer. At the bottom in the back left corner is a small box. Please bring it to me, hurry."

I unfolded my cramped legs, went into the room, and felt around for the item. I felt my fingers brush against a small leather box, so I gripped it with my palm and brought it back out for her. She just shook her head and closed my fingers around it.

"Open it," she said softly.

I paused, feeling the weight in my hand of such a small item thoughtfully, until she repeated once again with a firmer tone, "Open it."

I sat on the chair and cracked the hinge of the worn box. Inside was lined with dark green velvet, and there was a beautiful antique ring in the center. I recognized it immediately—it was her engagement ring. I admired it often, and she would tell me stories of how Romain had sold his prized colt to buy her the ring in hopes that she would marry him. How she was furious that he would give up something he loved so much for a silly ring. Together they would laugh and savor a moment so endearing it carried heat into the winter of their lives.

"I'm sorry I wasn't here when he passed, Raina. I should have been."

My chest began to rattle with a new rush of pain over one more way I had let down those I loved. Mr. Moreau treated me like a daughter, and I never thought twice about how it would have affected them both. I closed the box and went to pass it back to Raina, but she shoved my hand away. Confused, I tried once more, and was refused.

"Now this is the part where you listen to me, Stella." Her eyes were full of determination and, dare I say, fury. I had never seen her react with such tenacity, and was weary of what was coming next. I set the small box in my lap, and gave her my full attention.

"Before I die, you must know the truth. Julian and your mother were not going to tell you, and like always, I get to be the bearer of bad news. But I refuse to leave this earth with you believing one more damn lie. That girl that Heather saw, her name is Sgt. Shana Ficks, and she saved Julian's life. He was traveling with her unit, and their Humvee ran over an explosive. The truck flipped, and three people were killed. Shana pulled him to safety, and because of her, he survived.

"Julian knew that she didn't have a family, and he wanted to thank her by bringing her here to spend the holidays. He wanted it to be a surprise, because he planned on giving you that ring. The first thing that he said to me after the accident is that he knew he couldn't die because he had to marry you. That you were the only thing that kept his heart beating when the rest of his body wanted to let go, and she was the reason that he was able to do that. But he never got the chance to ask. You may think that once they know your memory is back everything will fall apart, but that's just one more obstacle holding you back from who you are supposed to be. It's not too late for you to make things right, so don't wait too long, because it might pass you by, and all of this will have been for nothing."

Hearing a car pull into the driveway, I knew our time was up. I tucked the small box into my pocket, then leaned over Raina, gently scooping her into my arms and holding her close. It was impossible to suppress the sobs in my chest as the broken pieces of my heart turned to dust. I wanted to scream at God for letting me walk through such hell, and in the same breath praised him for bringing me back to his place of reconciliation. Julian walked through the glass door and rushed to my side in fear that his mother had slipped away, then exhaled a sigh of relief when he saw her smile. Her hand reached for my face in comfort as I continued to fall apart.

Speaking with a newfound sense of contentment, she softly addressed us both. "I know what you are thinking, and it's going to be okay. Whatever happens beyond this point, I know you have found your way back together, and I can leave this world in peace. I am so very proud of you, and love you both so very much. Take care of each other. That's all that I ask."

The wheezing in her chest increased, and I knew she was straining to talk. She began to cough repeatedly, and needed to rest. Julian's body grew tense, as we watched her worsen with every passing moment. The nurse came in to check her vitals, and increased her morphine, allowing her to relax. Before she fell asleep, we both kissed her on the cheek, told her we loved her, and promised to do as she requested. Closing her eyes, she fell asleep content.

Feeling the small box in my pocket, I knew I could never look at Julian the same. His reluctance to fall in love with me became so clear, and I was devastated by the pain I had caused. I know that was not Raina's intention in telling me the truth, but now that I knew, it couldn't be undone. His face was sunken, with a shadow of unkempt whiskers across his jaw. He wanted to be strong, and although he had been prepared for this moment, nothing can truly make us ready to let someone we love slip through our hands.

I tangled my fingers in his, brought them to my mouth, and gently kissed his knuckles before leading him upstairs into the bedroom. He sat on the bed quietly, exhausted from lack of sleep. I knelt on the floor and removed his shoes, then turned back the covers. I crawled up next to him, wrapped my body around his, and vowed not to move until he awoke again. For the first time that week, Julian slept. Twelve hours of uninterrupted slumber passed before his eyes opened and he began to rouse. Feeling me lying next to him, he hovered over my side and placed a soft kiss on my shoulder.

"Hey you," I mumbled.

"Hey," he replied with a scratchy voice.

I turned over onto my side and ran my thumb across his soft lips, before leaning up and greeting them with mine. I was beginning to wonder if Julian was really going to leave me here after all of this, and I questioned whether or not he would ever trust me again once he knew my memory had returned. Would he be ever in fear of me abandoning him? I prayed not. Only time would tell what course our lives would take, but I continued to wrestle with my decision to wait until after the funeral to reveal the truth.

I moved the covers back to crawl out of the bed, but Julian's arm held my waist and pulled me close.

"Mmmmm . . . not yet. Just a little bit longer," he murmured, while nuzzling the top of my head.

While resting on one arm, I allowed the other hand to gently trace the outline on his chest. The small keyhole had never been touched up, and in the sunlight, I could see the spatters of where ink had not covered the skin completely. His beard brushed against my forehead, softer after a few days of growth. I liked how the thick stubble aged Julian and made him appear closer to his true years. Thin silver strands were woven throughout, and brought more light to his face. Noticing me paying particular attention to the unruly scruff, he palmed over it in contemplation.

"I like it," I said, while trailing my fingers from his ear down the length of his jaw. He gave a slight smile, then his hands reached below the covers and under my thin tank top. He cupped a breast gently, and his thumb swept across the nipple, drawing it tight. My body responded to him instantly, and he was driven by the feeling of my heart beating rapidly under his fingertips. He dragged his nails slowly down my abdomen, then began to nudge my shorts and panties down my hips with an unspoken urgency. He needed to feel something besides sadness and despair, we both did. If only for a few fleeting moments, we could journey together to a place of forgetting, the kind we should embrace and not fear, it would give us the strength we needed to carry on.

Consumed by adoration, it was in that place where Julian found me.

Although my memory had returned, my heart was still locked far away from anguish and suffering. I struggled with the unforgiving demons relentlessly. They had made themselves quite comfortable, and refused to leave without a fight. Clinging to Julian for life, I begged him not to stop. In a flash, I could see my body for what it really was—a vessel of skin and bones with an expiration date.

For we wrestle not against flesh and blood, but against principalities, against powers, against the rulers of the darkness of this world, against spiritual wickedness in high places.

Our greatest battles are not fought in the flesh, but with our minds, and our spirits. If we are bound within ourselves, we stand no chance against the external forces that threaten to destroy us—weapons, disease, abuse, or neglect. Of that which is earthly and that which is divine, we are all subject to the universal laws, but we are not without hope. As Julian sought refuge in the most sacred of spaces, I sheltered him with my arms and gave him the strength he needed to get through another day.

Love is patient, love is kind. It does not envy, it does not boast. It is not proud. It is not rude, it is not self-seeking, it is not easily angered, it keeps no record of wrongs. Love does not delight in evil but rejoices with the truth. It always protects, always trusts, always hopes, always perseveres. Love never fails.

Love never fails. Despite all of our human shortcomings and frailties, love never failed me, and my self-imposed exile from love was almost over. The last step was to walk through the door. I opened my eyes; they were blurred and warm, full of tears and devotion. Above me I could see Julian tangled in a conflict of his own. What distorted understandings kept him snared in a dungeon forged by a mistake? His torment was too much to bear, and I could no longer hold onto my intent. If I were to remain silent, the moment could forever vanish, just as I did years ago. He deserved this more than ever, even if it meant losing him to the truth.

I reached my hand up slowly, curled it around his neck, and lifted my body for one last kiss. He paused and matched my intensity with each movement, our tongues dancing feverishly against one another in a race to the end. Feeling him swell within me, I knew he was close and about to plummet over the edge. Fighting the urge to retreat, I trailed my lips across his face and into the crook of his neck. With my mouth pressed against his ear, I released my confession into the atmosphere and prepared for annihilation. Although it was merely a whisper, the words echoed loudly through his soul.

"I remember everything."

Chapter 23

~ Bombshell ~

Julian was unable to stop his body from reacting in both pleasure and shock. Adrenaline surged through him as my back slammed against the mattress while he quaked. His eyes were savage, and his nerves radiated forceful tremors. He watched helplessly as I shuddered beneath him in my own euphoric calamity. Time appeared to stand still as our breath and bodies recovered. The muscles in his jaw tightened, but he held me firmly in place. He was panting heavily, and I could see the questions forming in his mind.

"What did you just say?" he growled.

I refused to speak. There were no more words within me that could undo what just happened. Incensed by my silence, he rattled the mattress violently to be answered.

"I remember everything," I muttered.

Upon hearing confirmation, he pulled away from me instantly, as I had feared he would. His expression wavered between confusion and skepticism.

"How long has it been?" he demanded.

Growing indignant, I curled my legs beneath me and rose up. "Since the hospital. I didn't want to tell you. I wanted to wait until after the . . ."

Julian stopped me from finishing the sentence with a cupped palm to my lips. He was still locked onto my gaze, and I could see the turmoil starting to subside. I knew that his walls were crumbling. Before becoming too confident, I remained frozen in place. I waited for him to move, to speak, to take the next step. I had surrendered to him in every way, and what transpired next was up to him.

Understanding my vulnerability in the moment, he shifted calmly toward me and cradled the sides of my face. "You are still here. After everything? Do you know about Shana?" he said, bewildered.

I nodded my head and allowed more tears to fall. "I do, your mom told me everything. Heather was wrong. I'm still here Julian. I wasn't going to leave you. Not now," I cried.

He swiftly pulled me into his arms, and I breathed a ragged sigh of relief before allowing myself to collapse into his embrace.

"I knew she called you and that's why you left. I'm so sorry. I never meant to hurt you, I swear Stella. I swear."

His heart was pounding so hard I could feel each pulse against my cheek. Aside from the hospital, I had only seen Julian cry once. It was the night before he was deployed, and he'd shared his fears with me in the early hours of the morning. It was not death that he was frightened of, it was the thought of never seeing me again. No amount of reassurance could settle his heart of that uncertainty. Remembering what Raina had said, how the thought of me carried him through his worst nightmare, only to have it come true, shredded my wavering confidence to pieces. Over and over again, I began to wail.

"I'm sorry, Julian. I'm sorry I left you. Please forgive me. Please."

He held me tightly as my body shivered with remorse, and waited for me to exhaust all emotion before responding. "Stella. I'm not angry at you. I promise. I thought that you would leave again as soon as this happened, but you didn't, you're here. I don't know what to say."

We lay there a long while before moving out of each other's arms. I could feel my eyes swollen and itchy from the unending tears of relief. Julian smoothed my face with the palm of his hand, then placed small kisses across the bridge of my nose and cheeks.

I was waiting for absolution; I knew it had been granted, but I still needed to hear it. "Do you forgive me?" I asked tentatively.

Giving a mischievous smirk, he held the thought long enough to make me anxious. "Do you forgive me?" he asked back.

I closed my eyes and pulled in my bottom lip. I bit down hard, and let the final wave of uncertainty pass. Relishing the feeling of him so close, I opened them and smiled.

"I love you, Julian. I never stopped. Not for a moment. I loved you so much it nearly killed me. I couldn't live with the pain of knowing what I did to you and others. It was always myself I couldn't forgive. Not you."

Julian's brief smile vanished, and was replaced once again with melancholy. Knowing what awaited us on the other side of the door, I refused to spend another moment on regret. I pried myself from his iron grip, wiggled my way up to a kneeling pose, and leaned in to kiss him.

"We don't have much time," I murmured.

Julian saw the passion igniting in my eyes, then grinned and tackled me on the bed. Grief does strange things to people, but they do what they need to in order to press forward. For us, the connection of intimacy was favored. The passing thought of what the others in the house would think of our behavior at such a time was replaced with the devotion I held toward this man. Next to him, I could face any darkness, and for some reason, I was able to lead him through it as well. His caresses were more aggressive, as he devoured me with a new understanding. We both knew that there was much to discuss, but that would come in due time. Later, walking down the old stairs, we were greeted by the heartiest laughs. Ignoring it with a playful smile, I stepped over to Raina and kissed her cheek, then whispered in her ear, "He knows."

Her eyes widened, as Julian came up behind me and rubbed my back reassuringly.

"And yet we are all still here. The world didn't fall apart like you feared, did it?" she said beaming brightly. Confused by the conversation, my mother coughed, as if we had forgotten she was in the room. The thrill of acceptance was tempered by humility. I didn't want this to be about me. I wasn't the one who deserved the attention. I felt my chin quiver, as the truth continued to be a difficult thing to share. I slipped from Julian's embrace and sat at my mother's feet. In a way she would understand instantly, I repeated the words Raina taught me so long ago.

"Je suis á la maison . . ."

I am home . . .

Uncertain if she had heard me correctly, she looked to Julian and Raina for affirmation, before coming back to me in awe. "Ma fille douce . . ." she replied.

My sweet girl . . .

Overcome with emotion, she sank next to me on the ground and slipped her arms around my waist in tears. Whereas Julian had been my rock not long before, she too needed to let go of everything that weighed upon her soul. For all that I powered through, it was foolish to think the world would right itself instantly. Time had woven many layers over the years that would need additional time to adjust to. The human brain did not operate normally for an amnesiac in recovery. I often questioned over the past few months how someone could move forward when their entire life was on hold. Now I know, somehow you manage. You make a new life. You adapt to the changes and make the most of it, or you allow it to consume you by refusing to change. Of all the things we are certain of in life, only death and change are inevitable.

Julian sat next to me and wrapped his arms around us both. The amount of love in the room was so heavy I could feel it press down against my bones. We laughed as we separated, a mess of damp faces and sweaty hair. Then I used my fingers to wipe away the tears of joy, and glanced at Raina. My mom and Julian both watched my smile falter, and turned to where Raina lay. Together we stood and walked to her side. Hand in hand, we surrounded her. At 3:15 in the afternoon, Raina Tempest Moreau peacefully took her last breath, as she watched those she loved most seeking comfort in one another. Her face was content, no longer wracked with suffering, and her last words were a parting gift. Together we could face the darkest of nights without fear, by holding steadfast to love. Because love never fails . . .

My mother and I began to unravel the endless tubing and turn off the machines. The hospice staff remained distant, knowing she was in good hands. Once she was freed of her plastic chains, Julian tenderly lifted her from the bed and carried her into her room. Although she was gone, it did not stop him from saying goodbye and telling her how much he loved her. Doing my best to hold back the choking sobs, I sat on the edge of the bed and silently thanked her for everything she had taught me. She taught me how to love and accept myself, even when I didn't know who I really was. I arrived feeling like a monster, and learned to see with new eyes. The ink on my skin and the sins of my past did not define who I was. By becoming trapped in my own mind, I too was set free.

My father came quietly through the doorway and sat next to me on the bed. Then he pulled me into his arms, as my mother embraced Julian. After kissing my forehead, my father circled the bed to hug Julian, before saying his own goodbyes. In my absence, they'd grown even closer, yet another example of how God turned something so terrible into an act of love. I used to ask why God would allow terrible things to happen to good people, and for once, I understood. The tapestry of our lives suddenly took on a new perspective, and I could see our place in something so much bigger.

We were allowed as much time as needed, before the coroner was called to take Raina to the funeral home. At night, I snuggled close to Julian in bed, and we talked into the wee hours of the morning. He told me about his deployment, and how much he loved the excitement of the Navy. Watching his eyes sparkle as he talked, made me proud he stayed enlisted and finished graduate school.

"I wanted to understand you, Stella. I needed to know how a person's mind could become so lost they felt disappearing was the only way they could cope. I thought if I could understand how the brain worked, it would give me some sort of closure."

"Did you figure it out?" I whispered hopefully.

His arms constricted and he let out a deep breath. "Yes and no. I learned all of the physiological reasons why you did what you did. But I still couldn't understand. You are so strong, I refused to believe you could be shaken like that. And when you surfaced in California, it was evident you'd suffered some type of mental breakdown. I told myself that if I could find a way to help you, that maybe there was still a chance for us."

His honesty was raw and beautiful. I thought I was foolish for having the same hope. Julian and I responded very differently to our grief. He became constructive, while I went the opposite direction. Like the young boy who waited patiently on the dock for the day I finally gave in, he was merely biding time for the moment to arrive.

"What did I do to deserve someone like you?" I asked in wonder.

He responded with a fevered kiss, and I should have known better than to question my good luck.

"You trusted me with your heart. That is the single most difficult thing for a person to do. To willingly give yourself so completely, knowing that it might be broken. I knew it was a risk, but it didn't stop me from trying. I never regretted a moment of it."

I smiled and closed my eyes. Exhausted by the day's events, I placed my wrist across Julian's chest. "You trusted me, too. I'm sorry I let you down."

He hushed me softly, then held my hand in place and allowed me to feel the pounding rhythm below his skin. I could hear the crickets outside the window, the symphony of night, and allowed myself to relax. Being so tired made it difficult to remain positive. Ever knowing of my moods, Julian placed a gentle kiss on my lips and set my mind at ease.

"You are here now. That's all that matters, okay?"

I nodded in agreement. I had to trust that it was enough. I fell into a deep sleep, and found myself greeted by something I thought was lost forever. A dream.

The morning sun was bright and luminous. The vines were bursting like never before, heavy with fruit, and a light fog rested gently on the ground. Birdsong echoed across the valley, and a fox darted beneath the vines in pursuit of a rabbit. I laughed watching him race back and forth across the path, evaded by his prey. I stepped lightly along and told the fox, "You would be wiser to remain still and let the rabbit believe it was out of danger." As if he understood, he curled next to a post and watched the rabbit hop cautiously through the fog.

The trusting rabbit was unknowingly headed in the fox's direction, just moments from being trapped in the hunter's sharp teeth. I paused so as to not interfere with nature's course, and held my breath, waiting for the fox to leap out from his spot and catch the rabbit off guard. The cracking of a branch startled the fox and gave away his position. The little rabbit sped off up the hill, and the pursuit continued. Not wanting to miss out on the ending, I ran after them through the vines.

The fog grew higher as they raced into a ravine. Not paying attention to where I was headed, I felt myself collide into a low branch. I was knocked down to the ground, then the fog covered my body and surrounded me with an opalescent blanket. I felt myself out of breath and held my chest where the branch had struck. The little fox and rabbit were gone, and I was all alone. Suddenly, I was afraid and unable to move. Heavy steps moved in my direction, along with a familiar laugh. With strong arms, Julian reached down to the ground and lifted me up in his arms, above the fog. We were no longer in the vineyard. Loud waves crashed against the empty shoreline, and palm trees dotted the landscape. The water was a vivid blend of turquoise and emerald.

"I know this place," I proclaimed.

Julian smiled and set me down, and my bare feet curled into the soft sand. Delighted, I raced off onto the shore and dove head first into the water. I broke the surface, and was at the edge of my parents' dock, able to see the large striped bass and blue gills move about. Julian was gone, and the water was calm. Hauling myself out, I noticed that my skin was bare and small rivulets of water were trailing down my legs. My only thought was finding Julian again. Running up the back trail, I stopped just before the clearing and peered through the trees. A woman who looked similar to me was sitting next to my mother with an infant cradled at her breast. Her face glowed with contentment as they laughed and fussed over the child.

The glass door slid open and Julian walked out equally joyous. His eyes were full of adoration, while he bent down and kissed the woman lovingly. A sharp pain ripped through my chest watching him with her. I wanted to scream, but it lodged in my throat. I was frozen in place and unable to move. Before me, the baby was graciously passed to my mother for attention. Hot tears burned through my eyes and the excruciating hum of a violin began to play Canon in D minor.

My heart was falling to pieces watching the dream play out. I was a ghost. Was this the life Julian would have had if I'd never had the accident? It was quite possible. Who was I to be angry about a life I chose to walk away from? Unable to look any longer, I turned around and found myself in a stadium at the base of the stage steps. The crowds were chanting, "Protest, protest."

Glancing back down at my arms, I saw even more ink strewn about and wrapped in leather. I balanced precariously on stiletto heels as I walked slowly toward the top. I could hear the engineer give directions through the ear piece, though it was muffled.

"Two minutes until show time."

I cracked the heavy door, and the crowd was nearly deafening as it shouted for me to arrive. The band had all taken their places, and were waiting patiently for the show to begin. It was like clockwork. A small strip of dim lights guided me to the microphone. I grasped the cool metal base with one hand, removed the mic with the other, and began to tap my toe. The crack of the amplifiers incited more noise from the audience, and I could feel the electricity in my veins. This was my home. My voice was not trapped here. The vibrations in my vocal cords began to shift as though the words were lightening waiting to strike. Closing my eyes, I took a deep breath, and softly began the last song I wrote. It was supposed to be on my new album, the one I was going to release just days after the film festival. It was about him. They were all about him. And this was my goodbye.

Time has never been a friend of mine

The hours pass and leave nothing behind

I tried to stay

I tried to pray

Tried to tell myself it would be all okay but

I keep forgetting what it feels like to be loved

I keep forgetting what it's like to be the one

I keep forgetting every detail of your face

Maybe it's best, if I let you go

But I keep forgetting how

I let myself fall to pieces over you

The walls so high no one gets in

I hide from pleasure, hide from pain

Hide from love and I'm going insane so

Maybe it's best if I let you go

But I keep forgetting how

I keep forgetting how

Upon opening my eyes, I was no longer on the stage, but standing at the base of an elaborate altar. The wood was so luminous it appeared as if it were cast gold, with royal blue and violet shadows from the windows behind. Elaborate statues of the saints flanked the cross, and at the bottom was a marble statue of Pieta, the Blessed Virgin Mary. I was in Paris, at the Notre Dame Cathedral. I had come here after an exhausting concert, booze soaked and angry at God. It was two weeks before the film festival, and I felt my body starting to shut down. Going a million miles an hour, I would silently confess only an act of God could save me from myself. I paid my two Euros, by dropping the coins into the small metal box, and lit a prayer candle. Remembering my actions within the dream, I walked to the side sanctuary where the candle was located, and knew it was impossible to think it was still there.

My heels clicked loudly against the polished marble in the dark church, and a soft glow guided me forward. Walking through the massive pillars, I could see the wrought-iron tiers of red glass vases. Each one contained a small, unlit candle, and in the center was where I made my plea. The tiny flame was close to being snuffed out, but it still burned as brightly as it could. Not wanting it to disappear and leave me in the dark, I searched the space for something to ignite.

I reached into my pockets, but all that was there was the money I had brought to buy small souvenirs. I didn't care that it was all I had. If I didn't move quickly, I would be unable to see. I twisted the Euro in my hand, then placed it to the side of the flame so I didn't extinguish it. Once burning, I placed it immediately on the candle next to it. "C'mon, c'mon," I repeated until the wick burned orange and red, then sparked.

Looking around, I was no longer able to see the main part of the cathedral and became frightened. I needed to get out. I shoved the rest of the money into the box, then stuffed a few candles in my pockets, hoping they would be enough. I walked slowly toward the exit, and the small candle endured the journey to the door. One was enough, I made it.

The dream left me rattled and unable to sleep. So many things were etched into my memory, and I was overwhelmed by what it chose to recall. Although I had been sleeping, it was just as real as the life I awoke to. As much as I wanted to admit I was okay, and from a physical stand point I was, from an emotional and spiritual aspect I was still crippled. Hearing Julian sleeping soundly beside me, I realized the pain in my heart was real, and I knew deep inside he deserved a life I couldn't give him, no matter how much I cared. Julian had already sacrificed so much to care for Raina. It was unfair to subject him to a life of uncertainty.

Although we had found one another, the truth only amplified how different we had become. Our time here was a gift, albeit a double-sided one.

I crawled out of the bed and reached into my desk drawer to retrieve the small leather box. I opened it up, removed the ring, and held it up to the moonbeam shining through the window. Even in the dark, it glowed with a brilliant shimmer. Rather than slipping it onto my finger, I gingerly held it in my fingertips and looked at Julian wistfully. He deserved the doting wife and beautiful child. Raina was wise in her advice, and it wasn't too late for me to make things right. I tucked the ring back into the box, closed the hinge, and knew what needed to be done. I had to let him go.

Chapter 24

~ This is how we say Goodbye ~

Three long days passed before the memorial service took place. People traveled from far away to pay their respects. Raina's relatives from Alsace arrived the night before, and my mother hosted an elaborate gathering. While Julian was busy getting affairs in order, I went about with my own. The security team was ecstatic about my recovery, and an afternoon spent at the hospital while Brandon evaluated me proved revealing. The knowledge I thought was lost was easy to recall, and made the diagnostics move quickly.

Satisfied that I was stable, he questioned my plans and offered his own opinion. "I think you should finish medical school, Stella. I can guarantee you that within six months it would be as if you never left, and you have less than two years before you could seek a residency. Depending on your specialty, I could probably set something up here."

I smiled gratefully and appreciated the offer. Going

back to school was no longer on my radar, and I wasn't sure if I could handle the pressure required in the final stretches of obtaining my PhD. After being released, I wished him well and told him I would stay in touch.

"Just think about it, Stella. You don't have to decide now, but you are too damn bright to just let it go to waste."

I took his words to heart, but knew my compass was set to return to the stage. All it took was a brief phone call to my record label, and a new manager was being sought. I asked that everything be kept hush, and the PR agency was crafting a tale to work it to my advantage. Later that afternoon, I ventured into the attic to go through the belongings my mother had brought with her. Stashed at the bottom of a rubber tote, was my purse from the day of the accident. I brought it down, emptied the contents on my bed, and sifted through the assorted items. Expensive cosmetics, and several hundred dollars were tucked into the pockets, along with my tablet. At the bottom of the pile was a metal case with a few cigarettes and a lighter, as well as a small folded piece of paper.

Surprised that the purse was never searched, I carried the packet into the bathroom and lifted the seat. My hands trembled while I unfolded the corners and listened to the small granules scratch the paper. Inside was two grams of cocaine, pressed hard from sitting so long in the humid space. I flipped it over and dumped it into the bowl, then flushed it hurriedly and fell to the ground in tears. If I went back, that was something that couldn't go with me. It was a miracle my brain had not been more damaged between that and the accident.

I could not deny my prayer was answered. I made it through the dark. Money was irrelevant when it came to my survival. I just needed that one small light to guide me. The sullen mood was contributed to once again with Raina's passing, allowing me to get lost in my thoughts. I clung to Julian, knowing our time was growing short. The morning of the funeral, he dressed in a dark grey suit and plucked a few roses from the garden. My mother drove us to the church, and we found our way to a pew.

I forced myself to stay in the present and comfort Julian. His eyes were always far away, sharing in the same struggle of what tomorrow would bring. We listened quietly, hand in hand, as those who Raina loved exalted her life. Julian was the last to speak, and walked reluctantly to the podium. He had made bullet points on an index card so he would remember everything he wanted to say, and through the tears, I did my best to smile with encouragement. Pastor Williams stood nearby, and hugged him before concluding with a brief sermon.

"Every trial is a tool used to strengthen our faith. The book of James tells us to be joyful when faced with various trials, for it is a working of your faith. We are to allow it to happen, in order for our patience to be made perfect, so we can be complete and lack in nothing. Raina Moreau found joy amid her tribulations. As the cancer was ravaging her body, her spirit only grew stronger. She knew not to focus on that which she could not control, but spent every day making sure it counted. I can remember when she started her first round of chemotherapy and I came by to pray with her and see if I could offer any assistance. I ended up leaving with a box of pastries and a renewed spirit. There was nothing I could give her, other than what she desired most, and that was the understanding our sole purpose on life was to love one another . . . and for people to try her delicious croissants."

The church began to laugh, remembering their own

encounters of her insistence that no one left her presence hungry. Although I felt special in the attention and wisdom she gave, I knew it was simply how she was. It was impossible for her not to love, and she had passed on that trait to Julian.

Continuing the sermon, he took a note from Raina's book and left us provoked with a challenge. "As you leave here today, I ask that you honor Raina by emulating the life she lived. Think of what is best for others, and in turn, God will provide for you. It isn't always comfortable, because we are often selfish in our desires. But we are not meant to be self-serving. We are meant to live a life of sacrifice and love. Raina understood that more than anyone and every day she humbly lived out the word of God. Matthew 5:15 tells us, "*You are the light of the world. A city set on a hill cannot be hidden; nor does anyone light a lamp and put it under a basket, but on the lamp stand, and it gives light to all who are in the house. Let your light shine before men in such a way that they may see your good works, and glorify your Father who is in heaven.*"

She knew she was called to be a light unto the world. Each and every one of us in here today shares that same calling. Stop hiding your lamps. The world is dark enough as it is, and it is up to us to guide others. Go now in peace, and may the Lord be with you all."

With the service ending, the organ started playing a sweet hymn and the congregation followed Julian to the door. An endless row of condolences poured over him as I waited in the sanctuary. Before the casket was closed, I slipped up onto the altar and removed a small candle from my pocket. I placed it gently in Raina's hand, and fought the sobs in my chest from getting too loud. "It only takes one light to guide you. Thank you for being mine"

Hearing my mother call my name, I took a deep breath and kissed my fingers before placing it on Raina's heart. Since I was the last one to leave the church, Julian was waiting on the steps. I pulled him into my arms, and held him until he let go. Raina's wish was to be cremated and have her ashes released off the coast of Hatteras Island, so she could forever be with her husband in the deep. With two days to wait, we returned to the house and crawled into bed. Despite the exhaustion, I was afraid to sleep. Thankfully, when I closed my eyes, I was spared another night of dreaming.

When I awakened to a sun-drenched room, my clock said it was nearly noon, and Julian was already out of the bed. I walked into the kitchen, and my mother was seated at the table with her computer and a cup of tea. Peering above her glasses, she gave a slight smile and asked how I was doing.

"I'm still pretty tired. It's been a rough few weeks." I groaned while stretching deep, extending my arms up and off to the side.

"I think we are all a little down for the count right now, it's to be expected. I'm glad we have some alone time. I wanted to talk to you. Have a seat, kiddo."

Patting the chair next to her, she sounded upbeat, but I knew better than to think it was a good conversation. I went to the refrigerator and poured a glass of orange juice, then pulled the chair out and plopped down. She removed her glasses and set them off to the side, then closed her laptop. Leaning on her elbow, she gave another weak smile. With her eyes growing red, I could see the tears pooling.

"Mom, what is it? What's going on?" I asked with concern.

She used the cloth napkin next to her, and dabbed her eyes while looking at the ceiling.

"I just have to ask. I know it's only a matter of time, but when are you leaving?"

I reached out to pull her into a hug, and started to laugh. "Mom, I'm not going to disappear. I promise. When I do leave, you will know and we can Skype every day if that helps you feel better."

Nodding her head, she whispered, "I'd like that."

I rubbed her arms comfortingly, and asked her where this was coming from.

She took a cup of tea and shrugged her shoulders. "I went into the attic yesterday to store some of Raina's things, and noticed the tote I had yours in was empty. I had just been up there, so I knew it was within the past week. I was just scared I would wake up one day and you would be gone. I don't know if I could handle that, so I just needed to know."

Upset at knowing she was still unsure of me, I wanted nothing more than to set her mind at ease. "Mom, there's nothing saying that you and dad cannot join me. Even if it's just a few days at a time. There's so much I want to show you. So many beautiful places I have seen that I know you guys would love. Let me do that, let me show you. Just because I have my memory back, doesn't mean that you lost me. If nothing else, you have me completely now. I wasn't sad all the time. There have been some pretty incredible moments, too. You are my mom, anywhere I am, you are welcome too."

She smiled and I knew that was what she needed to hear, and over time, she would see it was true. Feeling at ease with things, she kissed my cheek and poured another cup of tea. As she pinched the sugar cubes out of the tin container, she started to ask about my plans for the day.

"Are you going with Julian? I'm sure he'd want you there with him, and honestly, I think you both need to get away. I sense there is some tension, but I don't want to interfere. I know you need to work that out amongst yourselves."

I took another drink and tried to decide if I was ready for food. I walked over to the fridge, cracked the door, and answered her while pilfering through the shelves. "Yes, I am going. I need to start packing, because I am sure he will be ready to leave as soon as possible. We are going to stay a few days on the island and decompress. I know we need to talk about us, and I have a feeling it won't be what everyone wants."

I picked out a cup of yogurt and some sliced fruit, set it on the table, and took my seat again.

"Stella, it's not about everyone else. It's about you, first and foremost. Do I want to see you with Julian? Absolutely. You are right, everyone does. But I also know that you both have lives you are eager to get back to, and those don't necessarily fit together. Asking one another to sacrifice more when you have already given so much is not realistic. You don't want move forward if you think it will be a decision you will regret. Perhaps, in time, that will be a road you will travel together, but don't make a decision based off of someone else's opinion. Give yourself some time. There's no rush to figure it all out right now."

I looked at my mother dumbfounded. I couldn't believe she would actually understand what I was thinking and feeling.

She smiled brightly and lifted her finger under my jaw with a laugh. "I get you more than you realize, Stella. After all, you are my child. Even from an early age, you explored every possible option before deciding on what path you would take. It's why you excelled. Once you had your mind set on something, neither hell nor high water could stop you from reaching your goals. It is also your downfall. But you know now life cannot be lived with blinders on. I want you to look around and explore all of your options before settling on one, because no matter what happens, I will always be proud to have you as my daughter."

Feeling my own face flush, I shook my head and rubbed my eyes. "We really need to stop making each other cry." I giggled while wiping tears away.

She reached over and tickled my ribs, causing me to howl. "Not all tears are bad. Even laughing can cause you to well up."

I squirmed in my seat and kicked the table, crying out again with a mix of humor and pain. She continued to laugh and poked softly at my ribs.

"Stop it, please . . ." I begged through short breaths.

"Do you know how long's it's been since I have tickled you, young lady? I think I have the right to make up for lost time."

Squeals of protest rang through the house as my mother pinned me down, refusing to stop her hysterical torture. Struggling to take in air, I didn't fight as hard as I knew I could. Finally exhausted after a few minutes, she backed away slowly, anticipating I would do the same. Neither of us saw Julian kneeling in the doorway with an amused expression.

"Hey," I said with a grin, then I flinched when my mother pretended to resume the attack. Together they roared with laughter at my scowl.

"Ha, ha, ha, very funny," I sneered.

Julian reached his arms out and pulled me up. I felt a tick in my brain, and closed my eyes briefly as I reflected back to the dream. *It was just a coincidence.* Meeting his gaze, I saw his brows draw inward with concern. Although it was brief, the reaction did not go unnoticed.

"You okay?" he asked.

Giving a reassuring smile, I nodded my head. "Yeah, I'm good. Are you ready?"

Obviously not convinced, he scrunched his brow again and nodded back. "Whenever you are."

Chapter 25

~ Plotting the Course ~

Julian was quiet as we headed east toward Hatteras. A friend of the family had a summer cottage in the village of Rodanthe, and offered it to us for the weekend so we could scatter Raina's ashes in the deep. In addition, he owned a boat that we could use so we wouldn't have to rent one. Julian figured it would take about an hour to pick up it up from storage and be where we needed to be by sundown if everything went smoothly.

We pulled up to the small grey home with multiple decks wrapped around the back. It was built off the ground to avoid flooding during storms, and was surrounded by trees providing privacy from the adjacent homes. If not for our particular purpose, I imagined this would be a wonderful getaway. The beaches were pristine, and absent of the high rises so common in popular tourist spots. We quickly went about unloading the truck, before heading a short distance to retrieve the boat. The yard had been called earlier in the day, so they had it ready and waiting for us to launch. We traveled down Myrna Peters road, past the Liberty gas station, to the small public boat ramp. With the truck backed into the water, I started the boats engine and let it idle until he returned.

Even in the sound, the water was choppy and Julian was careful to monitor the depths as it changed based on the tides. Once out into the open water, he shifted the throttle forward and began to speed diagonally against the waves. I held the backpack containing Raina's ashes to prevent it from bouncing around, and studied Julian's face. I no longer took his distance as rejection, and kept myself from prying into his thoughts. I thought about the conversation with my mother over breakfast, and pushed back the guilt I felt over letting Raina down. She had such high hopes for me and Julian, but surely she understood our plight.

I closed my eyes and relished the sensation of the salty breeze rushing across my face. It felt like it had been forever since I felt this way. Being out in the ocean was so liberating, and a tranquil way of paying our last respects. Half an hour later, we reached the coordinates where Julian had said goodbye to his father, and now he was saying goodbye to Raina. Handing him the backpack, I asked if he wanted to say anything, or if perhaps I could. He shook his head and removed the small tin container, then peeled the label off the rim that sealed it.

His hands shook slightly as he twisted the lid loose, but did not remove it. He tucked the tin under one arm, and reached out his other for me to hold his hand. Together we climbed over the back and settled onto the small deck. I rubbed his shoulders softly as he opened the container and tilted it to the edge of the boat. The water glistened with streaks of gold against the black water, the small fragments sinking quickly from the surface. He gave the container a few shakes, then twisted the lid and tucked it into his lap.

My French was not very up to par, but I was able to decipher a few things he then said. He was happy she was with Romain and no longer suffering, then there was something about me, and finally, he loved her. I had never been a part of an intimate death, so I wasn't sure what to do. Beyond the hospital and outside of my training, my personal reaction to it was strange and unfamiliar. I knew one day I would be doing the same thing, as an only child saying goodbye to my family. I couldn't comfort him the way that I would want to be, so I trusted that he would guide me with what he needed.

We sat and watched the sun sink beneath the horizon line, and the sky turn dark shades of blue and grey. The wind blew a cool breeze across the water, and caused me to shiver slightly. I wouldn't complain, so I just snuggled up closer to Julian for warmth. It wasn't long before he felt ready enough to leave, and squeezed my hand to let me know. He fired the engine, and we returned to the ramp with less urgency, then towed the boat to the house. Neither of us were very hungry, and opted to turn in early. While I found it somewhat odd that Julian turned to me sexually for comfort, I knew it was hard for him to verbalize his feelings.

It was in my arms he found relief of the burdens that he carried. I did not rebuke him for being too aggressive, or question his need to be held. A myriad of emotions surfaced and shifted with each caress, as Julian navigated his way through the night. In the morning, I would be forgiving of his methods of grief, and continue to assist in any ways I could.

As day began to greet us with a blinding light, I stumbled out of bed to draw the shades, but the top windows were bare, and allowed the rays to bathe the house in a soft yellow glow. Once awake, I was unable to fall asleep again, so I went downstairs to make a cup of coffee and sit on the beach. A short while later, Julian appeared, and took a seat with a mug of his own. He appeared rested, and listened to the waves crashing against the shore with me.

"I like it out here. Maybe this is where I will retire," he said.

I smiled, reached my hand out for his, and began rubbing the palm. "If you do, I hope you know that every morning you will know where to find me."

He tangled his fingers in mine, and they began a lazy dance of contentment. "And if I don't, where will I find you then?" he asked.

I paused my fingers, and turned my head to meet his gaze. "I suppose that is something we need to decide, isn't it?"

His lips pursed, and he was just as reluctant to admit that what we planned in our hearts wasn't lining up with our minds.

Understanding he held the same fears as my mother, I hoped that by addressing him we could come to terms with what would happen next. I squeezed his fingers gently, and chose to start the dialogue that we had been avoiding. "Julian, I know you want to go back to New York. You have never confessed that you held any desire to stay in Mooresville. The only thing that made you consider it was me. But even you knew that the moment my memory came back, I would have that same yearning to return to the life I left behind. I know that you love me, and I am not going to disappear again. I know that I have a long road ahead of me. Not just because of the injury, but learning how to deal with everything that has happened. You might be the most qualified person to help me, but I have seen you lose your perspective when it comes to me as well. I am not your responsibility. Leaving doesn't mean that you love me any less. You've sacrificed enough, and you deserve to be happy."

Just as I was bewildered by my mother's discernment, Julian appeared shocked by my empathy. I could tell he was having difficulty processing it, and had a hard time forming a response. I didn't press, and waited quietly for him to speak.

He chuckled into his cup and looked into the sky. "You know, I planned on telling you today that I wanted to take you with me, and I knew you would refuse. Honestly, I thought it was because you were afraid to leave, and I wanted to make sure you knew it would be okay. I would be lying if I said I wasn't in love with you, but then again my plans didn't include your memory coming back so soon. In some ways we know each other like the back of our hands, and in others we are complete strangers. I used to think if I ever found you again, and there was something to salvage from our past, that we would have this happy life and everything would be perfect. I should have known I was just dreaming."

My heart began to crumble as Julian sat up and started tossing broken pieces of sea grass into the wind. I couldn't blame him for the way he felt, I had my own delusions of grandeur. Growing restless, I stood and reached my hand out. "C'mon. Let's walk." I urged him with a slight tug.

He followed my lead, so I laced my arm over his elbow and directed us to the shoreline.

"I'm not saying I don't want to be with you, Julian. I just don't see how that is possible without one of us giving up our lives. I feel like I've been given this second chance, and there is so much more I still need to do. I would never be able to forgive myself if you walked away from something you loved so much, and I know it's going to take some time for you to trust me again. Aside from screwing like rabbits, our past is the only thing we have in common. We are both out of our elements right now, and we might find ourselves resentful if we don't acknowledge who we are as a whole."

I looked up and saw the corners of Julian's mouth twitch into a smile. I asked what he was thinking, and he bumped his hip into mine and knocked me slightly off balance.

The twitch broke into a full smile and he agreed. "For the record, I enjoy being a rabbit with you. But I also know you are right. It wouldn't be healthy for us to jump into something without all of our bearings, no matter how badly one of us has hoped for it."

I stopped walking and he took a few paces forward before realizing it.

"What?" he asked.

I held out my arms and twirled around in the sand laughing. "Hello. Have you seen me naked? What makes you think that you are the only one who has wanted this opportunity? I am a fucking mobile shrine devoted to all things Julian Moreau. Forever, mind you." I teased.

I grew playful, and I watched his pupils shrink as he took on hunter mode. My eyes grew wide and I began to step back in anticipation. Watching his shoulders flex, I knew he was ready to pounce, so I let out a scream as I ran in the opposite direction. I zig zagged along the beach at full speed. Each time I turned around, I would start laughing hysterically. He was undoubtedly faster than me, and this was sheer entertainment. He tackled me from behind, and I tumbled in the sand, braced by his arms to protect me from hitting too hard. Panting heavily, I was unable to catch my breath from laughing so hard. Julian had me pinned beneath him, and he started to tickle me.

"What's wrong with you damn people? Let me go!" I shouted.

Laughing heartily, he taunted me with a question. "What are you going to do about it, Stella?"

I tried to wiggle out of his grip, but knew it was useless. I was at his mercy, and he was taking full advantage of the situation. I continued to protest, but my pleas were weak. Growing tired of the fight and becoming immune to the harassment, I submitted beneath him.

"Ah, c'mon Stella. You have more fight than that. It's not like you to give up so easily."

I shook my head and grinned. "I know when to raise my little white flag. I won't win this, so I there's no point in trying."

His eyes took on an expression of satisfaction, and he loosened his grip. "Remember those words, Stella." He chuckled before leaning in and biting my bottom lip. "And remember when you are out in the world, how my lips felt against yours." He lowered himself again and gifted me a consuming kiss. I moaned into his mouth, and it only provoked him further. Sinking his hips against mine, he growled into my ear. "And never forget what it feels like to have me inside of you, making you cum so hard you almost can't take it, how I don't stop, and I make you cum again, and again . . ."

My body started to quake beneath him in ecstasy, as pleasure electrified every nerve. I felt his body lift off of mine, and opened my eyes as Julian was brushing the sand off his shorts with a smug expression. I lay there fully clothed and breathless, flinging my arm over my eyes in frustration.

"I hate you," I said with a smile.

For the next two days, Julian and I explored the island and each other's bodies with delight. We allowed ourselves to get lost in the fantasy just a little bit longer before coming back to reality. When we arrived back at my parents, he made the decision to stay at the vineyard, knowing his time there was also as limited. I offered to join him, and he politely declined. We both felt the pang of disappointment in knowing that soon we would be going our separate directions, and our beach trysts may have been our last.

I cried myself to sleep as I wrestled with whether or not we were complete idiots. I told Julian my plans about finishing out my tour, and he promised to see me when I played at Madison Square Gardens. I found a new sense of enthusiasm at sharing my world with Julian, and I promised to give a private concert at the hospital. I cried the next morning in my mother's arms, as I replayed the conversation . . . minus a few details. She smiled wistfully, but was proud of us for loving each other enough to let one another go.

"You didn't say it was over, you simply acknowledge that it wasn't the right time. If anyone knows that tomorrow is uncertain, it's the two of you. If and when the time comes for you to revisit the possibility, you will be much more confident in the decision of committing to a life together. It takes very wise people to recognize that they aren't ready or suited to live a life with someone else. I know it hurts right now, Stella, but it was the right choice. You will come to understand that someday."

I hugged her fiercely as my tears began to cease. I felt the weight in my heart finally lift, and the breath return to my lungs. I started to laugh and wipe away at my eyes.

Meeting my mother's loving gaze, I knew it would be okay. The next day Julian arrived to take me to the airstrip. A private jet was waiting, and he requested to see me off.

Christopher and Michael stepped off of the plane and greeted him warmly before addressing me. "Welcome back, boss," they said enthusiastically.

A young woman wearing a short black skirt and leather jacket stepped off of the plane next, and walked precariously down the metal steps to carefully avoid tripping in her spiked stilettos. All three of the men raised their brows as she approached.

Giving a confident smile, she marched up to me and introduced herself. "Miss Brady, it's nice to finally meet you. My name is Adie, and your agency has assigned me to be your temporary manager. I haven't had a singer as a client before, but I assure you I am qualified. The boys felt I was the best candidate, so I hope you agree and decide to bring me on full time."

I shook her hand and bit back a smirk. I wanted to elbow Julian, but refrained. "It's nice to meet you, Adie. I am sure you will be fine. These guys know me very well, and wouldn't bring anyone into my world that would piss me off."

Her eyes widened and she looked to Michael for direction.

He cracked up and placed his arm on her shoulder reassuringly. "Her bark is worse than her bite. Unless you are Julian. He would beg to differ."

She asked who Julian was, and he stepped forward to shake her hand. "I'm Julian. Remember that, because Stella has promised me all kinds of things, and it will be your job to make sure they happen."

I waited for one of the guys to crack, and commended

them for holding a straight face. I could see she was nervous, and I didn't want to start off on the wrong foot.

"Adie, were just kidding. If you are to learn anything about us, it should be that we are a sarcastic bunch. My favorite word used to be fuck, and I am well known for kicking random men out of my hotel room at odd hours of the night. Just know that those things won't happen anymore. The only thing that will stick is I am notoriously private and fiercely loyal to those I care about. As long as you are honest and take care of me, I will do the same for you."

She breathed a sigh of relief and started to relax. She tapped on her tablet and began to rattle off a list of my pending obligations before I stopped her midway through the second day.

"Do you mind giving us a minute? We can go over this on the flight."

Pausing in surprise, she lowered the tablet and excused herself from the group. I slapped Christopher on the back hard as he watched her climb the stairs and duck into the plane. "I am going to kill you guys. Really? That's who you picked for me?"

They both smiled and nodded in agreement. "She really is the most qualified. She doesn't mess around, but most of all, she doesn't drink or do drugs. You need someone like her to make sure you don't get caught up in things again. We've all seen it happen, and you have come too far. We promise to be good, we're just getting a good laugh," Michael joked.

I shook my head and shooed them toward the plane. They said goodbye to Julian, and left us to have a few words. I felt myself becoming anxious, and started twisting the fabric on my shirt. Julian reached out and stilled my hands. I would miss his cathartic touch, and the way he anchored me in place. Lifting my chin to meet his gaze, he smiled warmly.

"Don't cry. You will see me soon enough. This isn't like before. You aren't running away. If you need anything, I am a phone call away. Understand?"

I nodded softly, and tried my best to keep my chin from quivering. He placed his hands on both sides of my face, and I closed my eyes, waiting for his lips to find mine. Over forty-eight hours without his warmth had felt like eternity, but I survived. Just as I would the moment the plane left the ground. Noticing he had not moved forward, I opened my eyes in confusion. Julian was smiling mischievously, and placed a wet, sloppy kiss on my mouth.

Breaking away, I felt even more perplexed. "What was that about?" I asked scornfully.

He still held the same stupid grin, and I couldn't understand why. "If I gave you this earth shattering kiss before you left, you wouldn't be able to think about anything else. If I leave you with that, you will be slightly annoyed and pissed off at me. I have my methods."

He was right, I was annoyed and pissed.

"That's not how this is supposed to happen!" I shrieked.

Wagging his brows, he leaned in and placed his lips against my ear and started panting with an exaggerated heaviness.

"Seriously, kiss me, dammit!"

Trying to be determined and failing miserably, he gently cradled my head again. I kept one eye cocked open in the event he attempted something odd. I started to laugh, and knew this was going downhill quickly. He leaned in and hovered over my mouth, leading me to believe he was finished playing around. His lips roamed over my face, before landing softly on the tip of my nose. He released his hands, and took a step back.

"Really?" I asked, frustrated.

Bouncing on his toes ecstatically, he replied, "Really."

I shook my head and gave him the middle finger as I turned and walked to the plane. I heard him jog up behind me, then he grabbed my waist and spun me around, dipping me backward and laying another sloppy kiss on me. "Little white flag, remember?" he said teasingly.

I gave a knowing smile and nodded. He brought me back to my feet, and kissed my forehead before pressing his against it and looking into my eyes.

"Life is a series of choices, Stella. How we react will determine which direction it will go. Sometimes we make bad ones, even though we always hope to make the best. We work with the information we have at that moment. A bad choice only becomes a mistake if you choose not to learn from it. Just so you know, you were never a mistake."

I felt myself starting to cry, then he leaned in and kissed me softly, before pulling me into a tight embrace. "I love you, Stella Brady. I always have and I always will."

Choking out the words, I told him I loved him too. Knowing I had to leave, I reluctantly pulled away and walked slowly to the stairs. I stopped at the top, turned around, and looked at him sadly.

"I've made a lot of bad choices. I can only pray I haven't made a mistake."

I ducked into the plane, walked swiftly past the group,

and locked myself in the bathroom. Leaning over the toilet, I was helpless to stop the overwhelming sickness rattling my gut. It wasn't leaving Julian that brought me to my knees, it was the small leather box I set on his seat with a note tucked underneath.

Dear Julian,

There is a reason this isn't on my finger. It doesn't belong to me, and I don't feel right keeping something so precious. I hope that you find her, and marry her, and live happily ever after. I will love you until the day I die, but I know I'm not the one. You have my blessing, you can move forward now.

Love,

Stella

Chapter 26

~ The Next Chapter ~

Six months had passed since I left Mooresville and embarked on a new journey of self-discovery. Adie had connected me with a fantastic therapist who conducted Skype sessions, which allowed me to meet with her regularly. The first two sessions were mostly comprised of sharing everything that happened before the real work began. I loved that she wasn't afraid to challenge me, or intimidated by my status.

When I questioned her about it, she simply replied, "It is not my job to judge who you are. You pay me to help you figure out what is preventing you from being your best possible self, and empower you with the tools to move past any obstacles."

My mother told me right away about Julian finding the note, and how he expedited the process of selling the vineyard and bakery. When I asked how Darrick and Victor were doing, her voice grew quiet. "He didn't sell it to them after all. He actually chose a couple entering retirement to take over. They expressed their desire to have something to pass along to their grandchildren, and he liked the idea of it staying with a local family."

Although I felt Darrick and Victor would have been fabulous proprietors, I smiled thinking about returning to see children running along the trellises. I spoke to my mother daily as promised, even if it was only for five minutes. Julian had remained silent, but was in contact with my mother almost as often as I was. She didn't bring me up to him, and only answered questions when prompted. It saddened me to know that my actions would be taken so harshly, but we both seemed satisfied to know the other was well.

I was eager to return to the states after being gone for so long, and ready to unpack the unique treasures I'd collected along the way. I brought more than enough to decorate my apartment and share with my parents. I hadn't had a space of my own in so long, I wondered how I would feel coming home alone. But being who I was, I was never truly alone.

The plane touched ground at Charles De Gaulle early in the morning, and a chauffeur was waiting to whisk us off to the Hotel Napoleon near the Champs-Elysées. The concert was being held at the Parc des Princes the next day, and sound check was set for two in the afternoon. Since it was part of an annual music festival, I knew there were several bands playing, including Kai's. Word hit that we would be in the same city, and I received an email several hours later asking if he could take me to dinner to catch up.

Adie watched curiously as I primped for the evening. She never asked questions, but then again, I had yet to entertain a suitor. Flashing a devious smile as I left the suite, Christopher escorted me to Ribouldingue, an elegant eatery just a short walk across the Seine River to the Notre Dame Cathedral. My palms became sweaty, and for the first time in a while, I was nervous. Kai had attempted to reach out to me a few times since his visit to Mooresville, but I was never quite sure how to proceed. The two interactions we had were so tumultuous, it was hard to believe he still wanted to have anything to do with me.

The car pulled up to the curb and Christopher got out, then extended his hand to assist me. I was ushered into the restaurant, and immediately noticed Kai at the bar with his back facing me. After bringing my finger to my mouth to indicate silence, I tiptoed up behind him and wrapped my hands around his head to cover his eyes.

"Guess who?" I purred.

He turned around slowly and licked his lips, while assessing me from head to toe. "Now this is someone I remember," he said with a smile.

Setting his feet down from the edge of the bar stool, he stood to his full height and pulled me into his arms.

"Like you could ever forget me," I teased, as I continued to lean against his chest.

Kai chuckled deeply and leaned down to kiss the top of my head. "That, my dear, is impossible."

He put his elbow out to the side, so I slid my arm in for balance and looked up. Still wearing a blinding smile, he looked out into the dining room and nudged slightly. "Shall we?" he asked.

Like a gentleman, he held out my chair before sitting down. The small white tablecloths and wood paneling created an intimate atmosphere in the quaint space. The conversation was low, but jovial, as patrons dined; a few even accompanied by their furry companions. We ordered a bottle of wine and toasted to Paris.

Connecting with Kai was as easy as breathing. There was no apprehension, and our lifestyles had taken a similar course. Although he was under thirty-five, he had already set in motion the plans for retiring. Working with an investor, he was negotiating the start of his own business, opening an indie music compound in Los Angeles for new artists to record quality albums and learn the trade. He wanted to use all of his experience to pay it forward, and he knew that he could only play drums for so long before the band lost its momentum. The past year had taught him the value of being proactive versus reactive, because there were no guarantees.

I shared the events leading up to my recovery, and the challenges I continued to face. He was proud of me for seeking help and not feeling like a victim after the accident. While enjoying the delicious meal, I could see Kai's natural inclination to teach as he pointed out certain cooking techniques used to achieve the flavors. The painstaking process of cooking French cuisine was truly an art, and the food was to be savored. I would catch him staring at me a little longer than normal, and rather than being uncomfortable, I found a comfort in being free to be vulnerable. I mentioned the church, and asked if he wanted to join me.

He looked up over his bite of truffade . . . as if I needed to even ask. After finishing the evening with traditional croquembouche and cognac, we set off into the lights of romantic Paris, with Christopher as our shadow. The Cathedral looked more beautiful than ever, and I decided to share my dream with him. Upon entering the doors of the church, I was amazed at what my mind captured when I wasn't really paying attention, and could only fathom what details it was absorbing with intentional thought.

I stepped in front of the altar and laughed wistfully. "This is where I stood when I asked God for help, because I knew he was the only one that could save me. It was two weeks later that I met you."

Kai had been gently rubbing my back as I reflected upon the moment and started to weep. I turned my body to face his, and he reached behind my head and kissed me passionately. The bitter taste of tears was washed away by the sweetness of the caramel that remained on his tongue. Kai was breathing new life into me, invigorating every sense. He broke away and reached for my hand, pulling me toward the candlelight sanctuary. He pulled out his wallet, removed an American twenty dollar bill, and shrugged. He shoved the money into the donation box, then grabbed two sticks and handed one to me.

Before igniting the end, he bowed his head in prayer and spoke. "God, I thank you for saving Stella's life, and allowing her to be in mine. I thank you for this moment, and any more you can spare in the future. Thank you for also saving my life, and giving me a second chance when I didn't see one. In your precious name I pray, amen."

I wasn't able to stop the tears of joy or hide the smile on my face as he lit the small candle. Reaching out, I used his flame to light my own. I leaned against him, and watched as they flickered brightly. With his arm rested on my shoulder, we stood in quiet contemplation. He squeezed my shoulder, and nuzzled his chin across my head to break the silence.

"You said in your dream you shoved a few candles in your pocket in case you needed them, but one was all you needed to get out. I think what it was trying to show you was that, yes, you can get through your life alone. But the thing about candles, is that one can only brighten so much darkness, and the more that are joined together, the farther you can see. You were never meant to live in the dark, and you knew that. I think you need more lights in your life."

I smiled and poked his side. "Is that way of saying I should hang around you more?"

He laughed and poked back. "You know what I mean. But hey, if you take it like that, I certainly won't argue."

I looked into his eyes, and they were full of mischief, as well as light. I gave a flirtatious glance, and it was the only invitation he needed to claim my lips as his own. As if by divine appointment, the church bells chimed and Kai stared at me with utter devotion. How could it be that this man who I knew so little about was able to penetrate my very soul with just a look?

"It wasn't just the accident that God intended to use to save me, was it?" I asked softly.

Using the pad of this thumb to trace my lips, I felt myself starting to fall for him rapidly. I closed my eyes and leaned into his palm, willing myself to let go of any fear.

I felt him cradle the other side of my head and turn to whisper so quietly only I could hear, "For I know the plans I have for you, plans to prosper you and not to harm you, plans to give you hope and a future."

As Kai stepped back, I looked at him in wonder. He extended his hand for me to hold, and asked me the question I so longed to hear. "Are you ready?"

Epilogue

*The choices you make will dictate the life you lead,
to thine own self be true.*

~ William Shakespeare

"Dr. Moreau, you have to understand this is an extraordinary request. Hazel Rodgers has been a ward of the state for over twenty-five years, and now you are asking us to release her into your care. If at any time your arrangement failed to provide Ms. Rodgers all of the care she is currently receiving, we would have no way of readmitting her into our system. This places us in a very precarious position, where we may encounter future accusations of neglect. I am not quite sure we can take that kind of risk. We acknowledge the progress she has made during your time here, but we are only looking out for her best interest."

I sat forward in my seat and smiled broadly. I knew exactly what kind of argument they would come at me with, and I was ready to respond, but held back to enjoy this moment. For the past nine months, I had researched every possible option of removing Hazel from the New

York State mental facility, and had found only one loophole that no one could argue with. Due to the lengthy policies and procedures for acclimating a patient who has been deemed mentally fit to reenter society, my window of opportunity was closing rapidly. Not only had I accepted a new position as a psychology professor several states away, but Hazel was terminally ill and only had months to live. I cared for all of my patients, but she, in particular, made her presence known, and I refused to let her die alone, pretending she was insane.

And that was my loophole. Hazel Rodgers was not mentally incompetent. Quite the opposite, actually. She was brilliant. I noticed particular habits that were inconsistent with the behavior of textbook neurological illnesses. While reviewing her charts, I noted that her hysterical outbursts and erratic behavior only occurred just before her evaluations. Her history was very limited, which unfortunately was common with patients cared for within the system. Hazel Rodgers had a story, and I felt compelled to find out what it was.

In addition to feigning a mental illness, she was also not who she claimed to be. Her name was, in fact, Rosemarie De Laroux. She was born in 1942 in Biloxi, Mississippi, and was the only child of Geraldine and Robert De Laroux. Robert passed of a heart attack just after her birth, and Geraldine fell into a depression and died three years later. Robert's sister stepped in to care for her, and like her brother, suffered a heart attack, leaving Rosemarie alone at seventeen. She became employed by the aristocratic Collins family in Savannah, Georgia, as first a maid, and then a nanny.

Rosemarie cared for the Collins children, grandchildren, and great-grandchildren up until the family went away for their annual holiday ski trip. The winter weather had been particularly rough, and the small private plane crashed killing everyone aboard. In a flash, her own life was over as well. Not only had everyone she ever loved passed, but she was now forced to fend for herself. Beyond the archives I was able to discover, nothing more was ever said about Rosemarie De Laroux. It was only by chance that I stayed late last Christmas and found her sitting alone by a window with tears running down her face, while watching a family with young children leaving the hospital. No one came to visit Rosemarie the entire twenty-seven years she was a patient. She had written a letter once; it was labeled "return to sender," and rather than being discarded, it was placed in the large manila folder with her patient number scribbled across the top.

The letter was addressed to Charles Collins, the cousin of Beau Collins, who was the last grandson. To someone unaware of the family history, it would seem innocuous, but to a man who treated Rosemarie with such indifference after the accident and cut her off completely, it was a poignant reminder that it is important to trust those in your inner circle. Rosemarie bore witness to all kinds of family scandals, and not once did she tarnish the Collins family name. Her sense of loyalty was deeper than her hatred, even if it meant enduring hell. She only let her true feelings slip once, in a letter that I hoped would be the key to her freedom. That Christmas, I sat next to her and asked what was wrong. Proud and stiff lipped, she just shook her head.

Taking a chance, I nonchalantly asked, "Do they remind you of the Collins'?"

Her body stiffened and the tears stopped. Pursing her lips, she appeared as if she wanted to respond, and the long-forgotten devotion surfaced. She played her part well, even when caught off guard. Her eyes took on a clarity I had not seen before, and I knew in that moment I had reached her. Not pressing the issue, I went to the nurse's station to grab a handful of cookies, and placed them in a napkin on her pillow.

I walked back over to her, bent down, and whispered in her ear, "The orderly will be doing the nightly rounds here soon, and I suggest you check your room before he does."

I hoped that the sweets would be a sign of my silence, but only time would tell how much she would trust me, and why she didn't want to leave. I had been wrong in her willingness to be vulnerable, but it worked in my favor. I had to perform diagnostics and record data to provide to the hospital in order to prove my case. At first, it was just to establish her competency and get her the help she truly needed. After her cancer diagnosis, it became so much more.

Sitting at the directors meeting, I opened my laptop, and started presenting slides of my research. The placebos, the trials. She passed all of them with flying colors. When told she had an evaluation coming up, like clockwork, she went berserk. After close to three decades, I was amazed no one noticed the pattern. She was written off as a lifer, and only now, when the state was forced to reckon with how she had been treated, were they diligent. They were truthful in that they couldn't afford the negative press, because it would mean reform, and the system prefers as little change as possible. I knew they would say no.

The only way Rosemarie would be allowed to leave, was by facing her worst fears and being honest. I wasn't allowed to tell her why I wanted to take her with me, or it would be considered coercion. I knew she had post-traumatic stress disorder, and this was her way of coping.

Locked away from everyone and everything, nothing could hurt her. And she had been hurt; to what degree, only she knew. Hazel Rodgers had a long rap sheet of offenses that were obviously to get arrested, as she never harmed anyone or damaged property. It was always disorderly conduct, or resisting arrest. Once she was in jail, she was calm because she was off the streets and safe. It did not matter to her that she was surrounded by criminals, because when you pretend you have lost your mind, it can often be the most intimidating label of all.

After presenting my case, I waited for more resistance. I even provided numbers of how much money they had spent taking care of someone who was not actually receiving the proper treatment. If a rebuttal came, I would then threaten. I was no longer bound to the institution, and presenting my facts to the Surgeon General would certainly not bode well. Yes, I would go there for her, but I didn't have to.

Jack, the board director, took off his glasses and set them on the table while pinching the bridge of his nose. "Moreau, you certainly know what you are doing. My vote is to release her into your care, after she provides an admission statement, is made aware of her rights and understands she is leaving this facility voluntarily. You cannot be present when this happens, but we will inform her that you will be her power of attorney. Hopefully she will get the hint."

I let out a sigh of relief, thanked the board, and started to gather my things. Each of the men circled the large oval table and shook my hand, wishing me good luck. Earlier in the day, I was given an award of excellence and a parting fruit basket. Even they had a sense of humor sometimes. I wouldn't be able to sleep, thinking about how much this mattered to me. It was her choice to stay, and I still wasn't sure if she trusted me enough to leave. When turning the lights out in my office, I looked around one last time and said goodbye to the patients one by one. When I reached Rosemarie's room, I knocked gently. She was sitting on the bed and staring at the wall.

She turned to look at me, shrugged her shoulders, and looked away. "What'chu doing here, doc? Ain't you supposed to be gone by now?" she asked in her southern drawl.

I stood in the doorway, knowing I had to watch my words. "I wouldn't leave you like that. You know better."

She still refused to look at me, and stoic as ever, she hid her feelings in a vault. If not for my intense study, I wouldn't think twice about the way she tapped her foot in counts of four when she was upset, or breathed only through her nose, causing it to whistle ever so slightly.

I smacked the door and said, "Okay then," and started to walk away slowly.

Two steps out, I heard her yell angrily, "Ain't you even gonna say goodbye, doc?"

I walked backward, reached into my coat pocket, and pulled out a small napkin with several butter cookies decorated with sugar crystals. I set it on the pillow, and willed her to understand the message.

"That's up to you," I whispered.

She quickly snapped up the cookies and tucked them away in her lap. I knew I couldn't stay long, and I shouldn't have done it, but sometimes the rules have to be broken. No one but she knew the meaning behind the gesture, and I hoped it was enough. Looking into my eyes and knowing something was amiss, she slipped one of the cookies into her mouth, and nodded her head while the tapping of her foot stopped. While leaving the room, I could feel the crushing of the sterile facility, and was grateful I would be able to start making a difference soon. In a world where everyone is so quick to pop a pill and quiet a symptom, the root causes continue to fester and create an even bigger snowball of dis-ease in the body. Simply changing the diets of the patients to include adequate vitamins and minerals, improved behavior. But for the most part, my hands were tied, and I was forced to work within the confinement of the regulations.

I left the hospital and took a deep breath. This had to work.

The hours moved by slowly, and the hotel room became claustrophobic. I wouldn't be able to sleep until I got the call on whether or not I would be bringing Rosemarie with me. With the house sold, and the family already moved, I was alone in my thoughts and growing restless. I didn't like to drink to calm my nerves, but there was no other alternative.

The elevator ride to the small bar was quick, and a young server smiled while setting a cocktail napkin before me. "Can I get you something?" she asked cordially.

"A bourbon, neat please. Make it a double," I replied.

The amber liquid went down in a fiery gulp, and I raised the glass, asking for another. This time I sipped, as my stomach warmed and nerves calmed a bit. An hour passed, and I took one last swallow before settling the tab and leaving to take a shower. I had to try sleeping, because it was a long journey. In and out of consciousness I drifted, while waiting for the phone to ring.

At 9:14, I got the call. "Moreau, she's all yours," Jack said in defeat.

I raced to my truck and made the ten-minute drive in less than five. Placing my hands on the wheel, I forced myself to breathe and hide the smile. I couldn't appear too enthusiastic, or even get my hopes up until we crossed state lines. I went through the security check, emptied my pockets, and walked slowly to the discharge unit. Rosemarie was sitting in the lobby with two guards and a paper bag with her belongings, her foot tapping at a faster pace. Jack was there, and he handed me the clipboard with her papers, and a large file envelope with all of her information. A few signatures and a hand shake later, I walked over to Rosemarie and extended my arm to give her balance.

She did not question where we were going. Despite her attempts to appear placid, I could feel her body shake as we walked down the long hallway. A guard opened the door, and the sunlight hit our faces, causing us to reach up and cover our eyes. Rosemarie gasped as we crossed the lot, and I opened the door for her and helped her into the cab.

"What's this all about doc?" she asked nervously.

The hidden smile broke free, and I could see it reflecting in her eyes. "I have somewhere to take you. It's going to be a long ride, so I need to know if you are comfortable."

She looked around the cab and raised her brows. "If this be all you got, I guess it will work."

I closed the door and hopped into the driver's seat. I adjusted the temperature, and winked while hitting the seat warmer button.

A few moments later, she wiggled in her seat and laughed. "Now ain't this something! My ass is on fire!"

I reached out to turn it off, and she smacked my hand away. "I didn't tell you I don't like it. Just leave it be."

Raising my hands in defeat, I chuckled. "Yes ma'am."

The weather held as we traveled through the Catskills and down Interstate seventy-seven. We stopped in Harrisburg Pennsylvania, and pulled into an Amish family restaurant for lunch.

Rosemarie looked at the menu, unsure of what she was allowed to do, so I encouraged her first act of freedom. "You can have whatever you want. Even if you don't eat it all. This is only the beginning, so you better make it good," I joked.

She gave me a stern look, and ordered the fried catfish and a slice of pecan pie. As we waited for the food to arrive, she tilted her head and folded her hands in front of her. "So, doc, you gonna let me in on this or what?"

I was happy she was eager to know, and I wanted to tell her everything, but I wanted it to be a surprise as well. "Rosemarie—can I call you that, or do you prefer Hazel?" I asked.

She nodded her head. "You can call me Rosemarie, but you know it's been a long time since someone has called me that. I've been wondering how you knew who I was."

I knew I had to tread lightly, but I had to be honest as well. "I found a letter you wrote to Beau Collins in your file. I knew from the moment I met you that you didn't belong there. I tried contacting him, but he had passed. His son told me what he could about you." I left out the part about searching the Biloxy Public Library archives, afraid it might be too much.

She relaxed her hands and took a drink of her tea before laughing. "Glad to hear that son of a bitch is gone. This day just keeps getting better. So go on."

I laughed and shrugged my shoulders. "Rosemarie, we both know you don't have very long. I couldn't leave you there to die by yourself. If I can do anything in this world that makes a difference, I want to make sure you live out your last days being who you really are, and free."

Her eyes took on a damp sheen, but a tear did not fall. I didn't need a thank you. She trusted me, and that was all the gratitude I needed. Our food arrived, and she did not pry into more details about the journey. In between naps, she simply looked out the window at a world that had changed a great deal over time. We stopped at a hotel just shy of the North Carolina border for the night, so she could stretch her legs and rest. I wanted it to be daylight when we arrived. After a quick breakfast, we were back on our way.

A few hours later, we got off of the highway and took route twenty-one into Mooresville. We passed through the small town, and pulled up to the massive iron gates. She watched as I entered a code, and the gates rattled as they opened. The long gravel road caused my heart to race as we neared the property. I pulled up next to the back door, turned off the ignition, and looked at Rosemarie.

"Were here," I said softly.

The moment I opened the truck door, a bundle of energy raced toward me and into my arms. "Mommy, you're home! I missed you!" she squealed.

I gave her a tight squeeze, and kissed her face several times before she wiggled out of my embrace and crawled into the cab of the truck.

"Who are you? Are you the lady that's going to live here with us?" she asked matter of fact.

Rosemarie's face lit up, as the dark-haired girl with big green eyes was nearly in her lap asking questions.

"Ramona, please leave Miss Rosemarie alone and let her get out of the truck. There's plenty of time for you to ask questions later. Go get your daddy and tell him we are here."

As soon as I turned around, I saw Julian walking toward me with a huge smile. He wrapped his arms around me, and I finally crumbled knowing it was okay. Ramona grew concerned and hopped down, tangling her arms around our legs.

"Mommy don't cry. We made cookies for you," she said.

I leaned down and pulled her into my arms, as Julian rubbed my back, saying, "She's happy, baby. Everything is okay, I promise. Sometimes people cry when they are happy."

With Julian's assurance, she wrestled away again and stood next to the truck door, waiting for Rosemarie to get out.

I went to walk around, but Julian stopped me and kissed the top of my head. "You take a break. I got this," he said.

He circled the truck, opened the passenger side door, and introduced himself. As they walked past me, her eyebrows wagged, and I let out a slight giggle. We gathered in the kitchen, and I plopped down on the bench, exhausted, with Ramona in my lap, her head resting against my chest. Julian made a cup of tea for Rosemarie, and sat next to her as we prepared to share our plans. From the very beginning, Julian was supportive of my desire to bring her back with us, even though it meant living apart for a month. She took a bite out of one of Ramona's signature amoeba-shaped cookies, and praised her for how delicious they were.

"So, what do you think?" I asked while looking around the kitchen.

Rosemarie pursed her lips, unsure of how to respond.

"This is a mighty fine place you have here, doc. Your family is very nice, too. But I'm still wondering what I'm doing here."

I looked at Julian and smiled, before turning back. "We want you to live here with us. We want to take care of you, if that's okay."

She looked at us cautiously, and took another bite of her cookie. "Seeing as I have nowhere else to go, I reckon I have no other choice," she said with laughter. She looked at Julian and Ramona, and her face dropped slightly. "You sure this is what you want? It's been a while, but I am sure I can help y'all around here. I used to care for some children long ago."

Julian shook his head. "Rosemarie, you can do whatever you want, but we do not expect anything. You can sit on the porch and read, or go down to the lake. We aren't hiring you, you are a guest."

I could see the tears forming, and she fought desperately to hold them back. Knowing how proud she was, I set Ramona down and asked if she wanted to see the vineyard. She looked at me gratefully, nodded, and stood up. When we started walking slowly to the door, Ramona raced past us and into the field, then we made our way down the stone entry. Fall was coming, and the tips of the trees were a bright magenta. The vines were heavy with the last harvest, ready to be picked before the clouds rolled in and let the town rest. The air was slightly chilly, and it nipped at my bare arms, causing a shiver.

Rosemarie sat down on the plush garden sofa, and looked out at the lake down the hill in awe. "This is something else. How on earth did I get so lucky?"

Julian chuckled while rubbing my shoulders. "Maybe it's because you remind her of someone she knew long ago. Maybe it's because we all deserve to be happy," he said.

Rosemarie simply nodded her head and continued to take in the view. For the rest of the afternoon, she walked around the property quietly, learning where everything was and settling into her room. Feeling the quilt on the bed with her fingertips, she made a tsk sound. "This ain't handmade. I can fix one up for you real nice. I used to make the most beautiful quilts in Savannah."

I pulled out a flannel night gown and slippers Julian had bought in hopes she would be with us, and placed them next to her. "Like we said, you do not owe us anything. But if it's something that would make you happy, we can go into town and get some supplies for you."

She looked at the clothing and continued to feel the fabrics, assessing them with care. I knew this was a lot to take in, and only hoped she was okay. She looked up, and a rogue tear escaped, but she made no attempt to wipe it away. Since I was no longer her physician, I reached out my arms to give her a hug. She hesitated for a moment, and then allowed me to pull her close. All the emotion I kept buried, surfaced, and I allowed myself to cry.

She broke away, patted the side of my cheek, and smiled. "You're a good woman, doc. I hope you know that."

I nodded my head and left the room. Taking a deep breath, I wiped my face and went to kiss Ramona goodnight before going into the bedroom. Julian was sitting against the headboard reading, and set his book down when I walked in. He reached out his arms, so I crawled into his lap and curled against his chest.

"Welcome home, honey."

Home. A place that nearly slipped from my hands. I can close my eyes and remember the feeling of the thick envelope in my purse which I discovered while searching for aspirin the day I left. Crushed by the weight of telling Julian to move on, my emotions were no longer able to hide in the numb cloud created by drugs and booze. I had to feel each and every one of them, learning to accept that they were part of living. Unsure of what was inside, I was taken off guard by the contents. As I was in the process of meeting Adie for the first time, Julian tucked it in my purse while I wasn't looking.

Each page sliced my heart a little more until I reached the last one, a hand written note of his own.

Stella,
I can't believe I let you leave my life, but I have to trust that if it's meant to be that it will happen and I must let you find out who you really are, so you can be at peace. Just know while you are out there in the world, you will always have a place to call home.

Love
Julian

The small envelope seemed insignificant compared to the true contents. The bakery, the vineyard, his mother's house. Julian gave me everything. The color drained my face and I felt as though time stood still. Life as I knew it no longer existed and it was more than I could comprehend. Michael and Truman shouted loudly as the invisible branch hit my chest and I sank into the fog. Struggling to breathe, I closed my eyes and wished for nothing more than to have Julian reach through and save me. But he already had.

"We have to go back! I can't do this!"

Christopher ran to the cockpit as the others tried their best to calm me down.

"Stella, what's wrong?" Adie shouted.

Tearfully I handed her the folded papers and watched her eyes grow wide. She passed them around and several explicit words were muttered. Christopher came back with a mournful expression.

"Stella, we're about to land. The pilot says we have to register for a new flight plan and it could take a few hours. It's pretty late so it could be morning before we can take off again, I'm sorry."

He sat next to me and pulled me into a teddy bear grip as I gained my bearings. It would be okay. Julian would understand why I gave him back the ring. It was the same reason he gave me all that he did. My happiness meant more to him than money. For someone who lacked stability, he wanted me to rest assured there would be one constant in my life, always. Shaking my head, I knew I had to press forward.

"No, it's okay. I need to do this. He wants me to. It's the only way."

Michael handed me back the papers and I tucked them close to my chest. I clutched them tightly as I begged my body and mind to sleep for three nights straight. Like in the dream, it was as if the world continued to operate by no effort of my doing. The sound checks, the press releases. I just showed up and smiled. No wonder it was so easy to be high all the time. As long as I did my job, no one questioned my behavior. Except this was not some induced state with a limited time frame. On the fourth night, I would be stepping onto the stage of Madison Square Gardens for the first time in over a year. Tickets sold out in less than twenty minutes and legions of loyal fans were counting on me. A few rough practice sessions and it was as though nothing had happened, it was all some bizarre dream.

My dressing room was packed with flowers and gifts, closing in the small space even more. Surrounded by stylists and reporters, I mentally counted each breath, waiting to escape. Adie watched me wearily as did the crew, cautious I would suddenly grow cold feet and run. Placing the small plastic piece in my ear, peace washed over me and the earth returned to its previous axis. The crowds screamed my name, and I gave an inward smile as the lines between dreams and reality blurred.

Through the darkness I made my way up the muggy stairwell and to the stage entrance. Pungent smells of old equipment and pyrotechnics curled my nose and bubbled more memories forward. Like emotions, I had to let them surface and be revered. Waiting for the signal kick drum, I braced for the spotlight to shine in my eyes as I traversed the distance to my place on stage. Roars of applause rattled my bones and the heat of the flames bursting out of the cans by my feet molded the leather pants against my legs. The air was thick and humid as thousands of bodies packed the arena.

Foregoing an introduction, I raised my arm to signal the band to begin. We played a few fan favorites to open up and get me comfortable before digging into the new material. Muscles I forgot existed started to pull as I jumped and danced wildly, caught up in the moment. Looking out there were countless cellphones creating a galaxy of stars, and I imagined the cove. I thought I had been running away from life, when in ways I had recreated it on a different level. I was only happy when giving myself completely, and forgetting about everything else. My songs were the medicine I used to heal others and carry them through their own dark paths.

Knowing it was time to sing the title track, I scanned the front row for my parents to make sure they were okay. I had asked Christopher to stay with them so they weren't overwhelmed, and to my surprise they were both smiling. Piercing whistles echoed as the lights grew dark and the violins began the haunting melody. Music ran through my veins and I was about to bleed a symphony. It wouldn't be difficult to express the depth of pain I felt when I wrote the song, as the wound was still fresh. The most beautiful things are born out of the most agonizing of places. A crucial reminder of how short and precious life really is. It was time to set myself free.

I had nothing left at the end of the chorus. Giving everything I had, it would have to be enough. My knees began to buckle and I knew I would collapse if I didn't get off the stage. Blowing a kiss out and giving a bow, I was stopped the moment I turned away from the microphone. Adie was bouncing in her stilettos and the crew stepped away from their instruments to surround me. Scrunching my eyes together to decipher if they were betraying me, only a few more seconds passed before I realized what was happening. Dressed in a three piece suit, Julian walked towards me trailed by a spotlight. I started shaking my head confused and enthralled at the same time. Cameras had the entire scene projected on the large screens, inciting an even louder response.

Knowing I couldn't hear him, he took no time reaching into his pocket and lowering to one knee. Removing the worn leather box from his pocket, he cracked the lid and raised his hand to where I could see the pen marks that were wearing off from how much his palms were sweating.

was scrawled upon his skin. Julian reached out and grabbed my arm and placed my wrist across his heart, causing me to finally succumb to the weakness in my own knees. Not letting my hand go, he removed the ring from the box and slipped it onto my finger. I didn't have to say yes, and he didn't have to ask. It simply was. This was never a part of the dream, because I never allowed myself to see it. I didn't recognize the woman on the patio as myself, because I wouldn't allow myself to envision a future with Julian in it. Just as it only took a moment for my life to change for the worse, it only took another to reroute the direction I was headed. I wasn't sure how the rest of the journey would go, but I knew instantly I wanted him by my side. It was always only him.

A life with Kai was only one of several possibilities. A choice I could have made. Julian would have moved on, and as Raina taught us, the world would not fall apart as we feared. We have no way of knowing what tomorrow will hold, we only have the present to make choices that will hopefully lead us to what we consider our destiny. The key to resilience is finding a way to see love through the rubble of a broken heart and realizing it was only one vessel. You still have eyes, ears, hands and a mouth. Use them to guide you.

Acknowledgements

From conception to completion I felt as though an army has assisted me with this project. I started it nearly two years ago, and never anticipated how it would impact my life. It would be nearly a whole novel of gratitude to those who have given me support, encouragement, and the occasional honest conversation only a true friend can, that isn't necessarily nice but is best.

I always thank God in the beginning, because it is by divine province that I have this gift, to use my voice in such a way I can make a difference in other's lives. This is no exception. Thank you Father for all that you have done, are doing, and will do in my future. I know my steps are ordained.

To my angels here on earth. I know each of you has been placed in my life at just the right time when I needed you most, in different ways, but of equal importance. A thank you will never be enough so I hope this is a nice gesture.

Shana Shaffer-Ficks-The driving force behind this story. Life has dealt you a hand of cards no one would ever want to play, and yet you do it with such grace. You have taught me the meaning of resilience, and seeing love through the rubble of a broken heart. I hope this story makes half the difference in someone's life as you have in mine. I love you more than I think your realize, always.

Michael Gleason- One of my closest friends, occasional muse, and cover model. I may not always like what you tell me, but I do hear you. It's just selective. More often than not, it's because you are right, and you know I am stubborn. Thankfully I am learning to let others help me, and that I can achieve so much more with people like you by my side. You made me a better person, and that is real love.

Tammy Hanson- Thank you for reminding me of who I really am, and never letting me forget. From the moment I met you, I knew my life would never be the same. In a world that moves so fast, I am grateful you gave me a place of focus and peace, until I was able to find that in myself. I know we will grow old together. It's a good thing we have many years ahead of us, because it's not over yet!

Donna Sabino, Jodie Stipetich, Erin Knaus, and Melanie Hazard- Each one of you ladies could have your very own novel. I cannot count the number of times I have messaged you and said "guess what?" and each time you have been just as enthusiastic with the sheer insanity of the idea. You have given me hours of your life in order to help me write the best stories I possibly can, as well as giving me the strength to reshape my own. To know that you put your very hearts and souls into this community makes me humbled and proud to have you as friends, and grateful for this journey.

Nichele Fabrizio- It is because of you I first hit the publish button, and time and time again you have pushed me past my comfort zone. Thank you for helping me to polish Forgetting and understanding how I tell a story. Now is my time to return the favor, because this is where you were meant to be.

Rome Ntukogu- After years of building a friendship, we are embarking on a new venture of building dreams. You have supported everything I have done since day one, from the first sermon I ever preached, to the grassroots of my career as an author. You have been not just a mentor, but a rock in which I knew I could always rely on. We will do great things, I know it, and this is just the beginning.

My editor Jennifer Sell, formatter Tami Norman at Integrity, and my graphic designer and photographer Heather McHenry at MHMPhotography. Your brilliant talents and hours of grueling work to shape this story has not gone unnoticed. You each know how important it was to me, and made sure to give it your best as well. I just write the words, you help me make them into a masterpiece I will treasure forever.

Stephanie DeLamater Phillips- Although we have never met, you have touched my life in such an amazing way. From the radio show introducing me to Mylee YC, to the blog tour, I admire that you use your voice to help others. Thank you for stepping in when I needed you most, and helping me to share this story with the world. Stephanie's Book Reports folks!

Brandon Perry- You are such an inspiration with your groups Ollie's Kids and Good Samaritans, but it's your work with the Beat It 5k that has impacted me the most. Thank you for introducing me to Dr. Tuohy, and sharing the importance of letting the world know about his work. Together we will get the message out! I love and adore you, thank you for being a part of my story.

Nick Sabatalo- I must thank Nichele, because she is the one who helped me find you. I was looking for a cover model, and instead I was given a fantastic partner in crime. Your talent and drive was so admirable, and your humor never ceases to catch me off guard. I love how I have been able to watch you grow in your own talent, as you have endlessly encouraged me in mine. You deserve the best.

Darrick Beekman- I would have never guessed an evening out would have turned into a wonderful friendship by chance encounter. I am honored and blessed you allowed me to use you in my story, now we need to get yours going next. This will happen!

And last but not least, my family and friends. I cannot list you all, but you know who you are. I could not do this without your encouragement and love. Thank you for reading my stories as I write them, and being patient as I rattle off a million miles an hour. They say you are known by the company you keep, so I must be pretty amazing because I am surrounded by greatness.

Love always, until next time…

JL Brooks

About the Author

JL Brooks is a former columnist turned novelist. What started as a bet changed her entire course in life. With a passion for adventure, she believes everyone has a story to tell. Chances are she will try to convince you to tell yours.

Follow JL at

Twitter: @Authorjlbrooks

Facebook: www.facebook.com/authorjlbrooks

Email: Authorjlbrooks@gmail.com